The

Obscured Journey

Rise
from the
Fog
of
Uncertainty

Jerald Albritton

Copyright © 2019 to Jerald Albritton. Use of any part of this book without permission from the author, their representatives or agents is prohibited by law. All Rights reserved. No part of this book may be reproduced, transferred, modified, or used in part in any way and in any form without the express written consent of the author, agents or representatives.

Published in the United States
The Obscured Journey - Rise from the Fog of Uncertainty
Copyright © 2019 Jerald Albritton
First Edition, December 2019
ISBN: 978-1-7343583-6-0

My Uncle Delwin had a stroke early in his life which handicapped him for a while yet he still smiles and laughs every time I see him. My uncle gave me the best thing a person can give you which is belief. He always believed in me no matter what I did. Even when I did ignorant things, he still had faith that I would learn and stay on the right track. I love you Unc and I wouldn't be who I am without you. You mean more to me then you probably ever understood. The battles you fought for me that you might not remember, or even recognize, have stayed in my heart to this day. Thanks for being my light at times when I didn't think I needed it. This book is **DEDICATED** to you Unc. I'll never forget when you told me that "You can pout about the choices or you can make the best out of the choices you have made."

"The hardest thing to do is to be true to yourself, especially when everybody is watching."

- *Dave Chappelle*

Dedication
Epigraph
A Note from Jerald II
Preliminary III

PART I POTENTIAL X POSSIBILITIES 1

| Chapter 1 | Dare to Question 2
| Chapter 2 | Societal Interpretations 17
| Chapter 3 | Mark of the Chosen 21
| Chapter 4 | What Steers You? 28
| Chapter 5 | Dream Unimaginably 44

PART II AWAKENING X ACKNOWLEDGEMENT .. 55

| Chapter 6 | Lost Connections 56
| Chapter 7 | Imprisoned Illusions 75
| Chapter 8 | Bearing the Risk 101
| Chapter 9 | Leverage your Anguish 115

PART III TRANQUILITY X THRIVE 139

| Chapter 10 | Retrofitting the Mind 140
| Chapter 11 | Formidable Challenge 161
| Chapter 12 | Resolve 180

PART IV HUMANITARIAN X HIGHLIGHT 199

| Chapter 13 | Engulfed by Entiltlement 201
| Chapter 14 | Eyes of the Immortal 210

Coda 213
Write your own Notes 218
Acknowledgments 225
Week Paid Vacation 228
Author's Short Story 229
About the Author 242

A Note from Jerald

In this world full of greed, unlove, hate, suffering, unfairness and uncertainty, it is prudent to be at peace not only with yourself externally, but internally as well. The best thing about living is that we have the power of choice. We can either let our circumstances destroy us, define us or strengthen us. Ultimately, the decision is ours. Would you rather be at peace with yourself and at war with the world or would you rather be at peace with the world and at war with yourself? As elegantly asked by Nipsey Hussle. We always say, "Rest in peace"—well why don't we say, "Live in peace," as well?

What we can or cannot do, what we consider possible or impossible, is rarely a function of our true ability. It is more likely a function of our beliefs about who we are. Our belief system can give us the power to overcome and move forward pass barriers we could never fathom. When everything feels like an uphill battle, just think of the view once you reach the top.

Anything in life fortune has brought you, count it as a lost already because it was never yours to begin with. Nothing is permanent in this corrupt/wicked world not even our troubles. My hope is that this book will help you find courage, strength, and wisdom to make the best decisions possible for you. I ask that you start today by living the way you wish to be remembered by on your journey.

Jerald Albritton

Preliminary

An Invitation

I wrote this book with the intention of helping millennials like me answer some questions that I've had. I've realized that even once we get older the feeling of what's next can seep in so this book is for all that wish to discover the next chapter of their life. It's taken me a while to get here with a lot of pain and great lessons learned. I can't teach you the lessons because that's something we all have to do on our own. What I can do is share the tools and knowledge I use, to walk on my journey.

I want you to grasp what chapters hit you hard and those that do not. Later in life you may realize a chapter that was irrelevant at first become relevant to your everyday lifestyle. We constantly change through our trials and tribulations, slowly becoming who we were meant to be or who we were meant to help catapult. True Change cannot be made if it is bound by laws, limitations, predictions and imagination.

> *"People who can't throw something important away can never hope to change anything."*
>
> *Amir Alert (Hajime Isayama)*

Quiet the mind and go within. Cease looking to the world to define you. The answers, the path, the real deal is behind every breath you take, watching and waiting for you to finally look in the right direction, only when you perceive your own inner power and beauty, can you truly see the same in the world clearly.

Before chapter one, I want you to go to a special place filled with beautiful scenery. That could be a beach, the top of a mountain, near a lake, a park or wherever you think is most beautiful. Mother Nature is elegant and is great for achieving peace of mind. While you're there, I want you to turn your phone on silent and just think about your life. Think about when you were a kid, think about when you were a teenager, and think about how you are now. Although it may be tough, you can be honest with yourself because these are your thoughts, this is your life and you're in your own world. Like woody and buzz lightyear said, reach for the sky, to infinity and beyond.

Part I

Potential

X

Possibilities

Chapter 1

Dare to Question

"To have faith is to trust yourself to the water. When you swim you don't grab hold of the water, because if you do you will sink and drown. Instead you relax, and float"

- *Alan Watts*

Philosophical Discovery

Few people question the depth and meaning of life. Obviously, you are one of them as you've chosen to read a book that presents an approach to understanding. Below is a list of questions that few people can answer as they've never considered the questions. There are no right or wrong answers—we are all different, and our answers come from our personal perspectives. See what you answer now then answer them again when you've completed reading the book. Did any of the answers change? (Write your answers in the notes section located in the back. When you finish reading the book, compare your answers now to how you feel when you've finished reading the book. See if they have changed.)

- What attachments can't I let go of, and can I live without these earthly attachments?
- What is out there that you would jeopardize your life to protect?
- Do you still harbor guilt from any event in your life, if so, why?
- What is my purpose or reason for being in this world?
- What illusions do I continue to uphold, and why?
- What are some of the lies that I tell myself?
- What grief have I not been able to forgive?
- What would others say at my funeral?
- What are you ashamed of, and why?
- What are you most afraid of?
- What are my core values?
- What do I hate?

We all have the freedom to find answers. The above questions require we search ourselves and our experiences. We aren't going to find them online or in reference books. They come to us through our experiences and perceptions. Sometimes the answers are based in gentle memories, and sometimes they are based in pain. To achieve honest answers requires we are honest with ourselves. American songwriter and musician Henry Rawlins once wrote, "Sometimes the truth hurts"[1]—in seeking the answers, you will find pain.

Finding your truth is a journey, and as with all journeys comes pleasure and pain. In order to grow, we must allow ourselves to go through all the emotions generated by any given situation. In an article printed in Psychology Today, Jennifer Rollins states, "Rather than trying to suppress your feelings, work to be a mindful observer of them. Notice the emotions that you experience and where you feel them in your body. Then, try to cultivate a curious and nonjudgmental stance. Our emotions are often messengers, which signal something important that we need to pay attention to."[2] Allowing ourselves to experience the emotions allows us to find our truths. In seeking answers, don't turn away from the painful, embrace the emotions, and grow from them.

---

[1] "Henry Rollins Quotes." BrainyQuote.com. BrainyMedia Inc, 2019. 15 May 2019. https://www.brainyquote.com/quotes/henry_rollins_381416

[2] Jennifer Rawlins; Psychology Today.com, 2016. 25 November 2016 https://www.psychologytoday.com/us/blog/mindful-musings/201611/3-reasons-let-yourself-feel-your-emotions

> *"Life is never made unbearable by circumstances, but only by lack of meaning and purpose."*
>
> *- Viktor Frankl*

When we find meaning in our suffering or pain, we find the strength to go on—to keep moving forward. That meaning can be anything that is significant to us, whether that means moving toward a goal, enriching our lives, or making someone smile. In doing so, we begin to live our lives and not just exist.

To Live, really live, is rare. Most people just exist. They survive. They continue to breathe. Many people don't know themselves. This situation isn't isolated to young adults. The world is filled with definitions, expectations, and beliefs that bombard us. As young adults are, however, we are particularly affected as we are still trying to define who we are, who we want to be, and how to get there. We have an infinite amount of influences, and there are always those who try to guide us yet have no real map. These mapless guides are typically trying to take us down their paths versus guiding us to find our own.

Knowing who we are is the first step in finding our path. We need to understand what our strengths are as well as our weaknesses. This knowledge will lead us to what we want to accomplish in life. Think of it as a steppingstone. Each stone we set, builds our path. Before we begin to build the path, we must decide not to be complacent.

Hidden Strength

> *"The very basic core of a person's living spirit is his passion for adventure. The joy of life comes from our encounters with new experiences, and hence there is no greater joy than to have an endlessly changing horizon, for each day to have a new and different sun."*
>
> *- Christopher McCandless*

Complacency is defined as "self-satisfaction, especially when accompanied by unawareness of actual dangers or deficiencies."[3] In this context, the 'dangers or deficiencies' refer to not looking at who you are or caring who you want to be. You live someone else's agenda for you. This situation often leads to the 'pity-party,' victim response. "Life isn't fair." "I deserve more." "It should be given to me." These attitudes can deplete your strength and rob you of your dreams.

You can bemoan the situation you find yourself in, and say that it isn't fair—that you deserve everything to be easier. But, is that what you really want? Do

---

[3] https://www.merriam-webster.com/dictionary/complacency

you want to say that you are happy because everything was handed to you, or do you want the strength to defeat the odds and claim what makes you happy yourself?

> *"Nothing worse than being strong, but not strong enough."*
>
> *- Shinobu Sensui (Yoshihiro Togashi)*

If you are going to do great things, you need strength. To have strength, you need a good foundation to build your strength on. The example I give is in building a beach house on one piling—a powerful wave can wash it away and the house will crumble. But, build it on four pilings, and one is washed away, the house will stand. The same is true for building ourselves. If we do not have a solid foundation, that wave—in this case, the "victim/pity party" approach—will wash away our foundation, and we will be lost.

Foundation is defined as a basis (such as a tenet, principle, or axiom) upon which something stands or is supported.[4] Given that definition, what is our foundation? Where does it come from? It comes from our beliefs. I grew up reading scriptures and

---

[4] https://www.merriam-webster.com/dictionary/foundation

going to church, therefore my foundation is God. It is what I believe.

Paradox of Beliefs

Meriam and Webster define belief as a state or habit of mind in which trust or confidence is placed in some person or thing.[5] For example: her *belief* in God; a *belief* in democracy, or perhaps, I bought the chest of drawers in the *belief* that it was an antique. These beliefs are formed by our acceptance of what people have told us or by experience and reflection. The difficulty comes in what is really true. Because someone has told us something does not make it true. By the same token, when we reflect on our experiences, we are biased, so is our conclusion correct? Not a simple question.

In science, something is deemed qualified through its repeatability and quantified by an equation. Special Relativity is quantified by $E=mc^2$. This equation means Energy is equivalent to mass (m) x velocity^2 (c). C is the constant representing the speed of light. In 1905 the speed of light was accepted as 186,000 miles per second. Experiments at CERN laboratory in Switzerland showed that a

---

[5] https://www.merriam-webster.com/dictionary/belief

neutrino traveled from there to Italy 60 billionth of a second faster than the speed of light.[6] Does this mean that what Einstein postulated isn't true? No. It proves that things change and beliefs shift.

Some scientist finds this difficult to believe because of its implications, however, many are fascinated. This isn't a physics lesson, so I won't get into the implications. What I am trying to illustrate here is that not everyone believes the same things even with proof.

As we formulate our beliefs, it is important to know that it's ok not to share or agree with someone else's beliefs as it is acceptable for people not to share yours. The lesson is not to allow others to dictate what is right or wrong for you. People who believe in God are no different from people who believe in things that they have read or seen, which was created by somebody they have never met. Whatever it is you believe in, make sure it helps aid in who you are.

If somebody disagrees with you, then so be it. Everyone doesn't need to be in agreement with you

---

[6] Wynne Parry; Live Science; Why the Speed of Light Matters; 26 November 2011; https://www.livescience.com/16248-speed-light-special-relativity-neutrinos.html

for you to achieve your goals or what it is that you want to accomplish on this earth. Most people go with the majority to not feel alienated despite what they have seen. In some cases, the majority isn't always the best way example to follow. Our opinions are more often formed from questionable sources on the internet or even in news broadcasts. These sources are not always objective and try to sway us in one direction or the other. Without verifying the facts for ourselves, we have little way to tell what reality versus fiction or propaganda is. Have the strength of your convictions and be cautious where you base your faith in information.

Science continues to develop new theories, while some older theories are set aside. The classic example here would be that Newton proved Galileo wrong, who in turn proved Aristotle wrong. Here the theory evolved from one physicist to the next. Were they wrong to begin with? No, they saw the problem differently and had more information to work with. The same principle can be applied to our beliefs. Formulating our beliefs should come from multiple sources, but we should also be open to having our opinions evolve.

Believe in what you want despite what people say. We would rather live thinking everything is ok then know the truth. We feel fine but don't want to go to the doctor in fear that something may be wrong. There are those who have mastered the art of perception, so don't always believe things that tend to be true. Live your life, and go with what you feel is right. Live by what you feel and think not by what you have been told to think despite who tells you whether that be your friend, teacher, parent, or boss. Don't be brainwashed. If you feel differently, then speak up or ask questions. Be true to yourself—who you feel you are not, what others think you should be. Shakespeare wrote one of the greatest lines in Hamlet that says: "To thine own self be true."[7] How appropriate that statement.

Our beliefs are what make us who we are. It doesn't matter what those beliefs are. You may believe a lie, but that lie is your reality. You may be atheist, but that doesn't make you wrong, or evil as some would tell. What it makes you is different. You believe in something different. That does not make it wrong. We are individuals with our own experiences that formulated our ideas. Because someone doesn't

---

[7] William Shakespeare; Hamlet; Circa 1600

believe the way we do, does not make them wrong either. Remember, we were created equally, and each have our skills and talents.

It is also important to be open to other ideas. Listen. Don't judge or criticize. Doors open when we listen. Be adventurous enough to walk through that door. Once it closes, it may never open again. Don't be left wondering what if or wishing you could step back in time and walk through that door. While we learn from the past, we cannot go back and change it. If we are not willing to entertain new ideas, then we become complacent and can easily stagnate.

> *"The real voyage of discovery consists not in seeking new lands but seeing with new eyes."*
>
> *- Marcel Proust*

Believability—how do we define that? Believing something can come from hard proof as in seeing something happen or it can come from faith, knowing that it did from some visceral response within ourselves. Love is real, yet it is difficult to believe in because of the great pain it can cause. Ask any lover. The universe is hard to believe. There are so many things we cannot see, yet they are there. Ask a scientist.

Our beliefs come from a variety of sources—educators, parents, clergy, books, newspapers, magazines, as well as rumors, myths, and legends. Those beliefs formulated from 'verifiable' sources are easy to justify. We can do tangible research with qualified results. The question is, how do we discern between the latter three influences in terms of truth?

First, we have to look at how each is defined. Rumor can be a noun or a verb. As a noun ,it is defined as talk or opinion widely disseminated with no discernible source or as a statement or report current without known authority for its truth.[8] As a verb: be circulated as an unverified account or to tell or spread by rumor.[9] One of the most famous rumors in the 1920s-1930s was that alligators lived in the sewers of New York City. It was said that New Yorkers visiting Florida would bring home baby alligators as souvenirs. When they grew too big, they would flush them down. Was this true? Well, of course not. An alligator would not survive the frigid winter temperatures of New York; they are a warm climate animals. Not to mention, that no

---

[8] https://www.merriam-webster.com/dictionary/rumor
[9] See 9

creature would survive long navigating in sewage. Rumors can be proven or disproven.

> *"Through action, a man becomes a Hero. Through death, the Hero becomes a Legend. Through time, the Legend becomes a Myth. And by learning from the myth, a man takes action."*
>
> - *Corazon (Eiichiro Oda)*

A myth is defined as something that is usually a traditional story of ostensibly historical events that serves to unfold part of the world view of a people or explain a practice, belief, or natural phenomenon or a belief that embodies the ideals and institutions of a society or segment of society. Most interestingly, it is defined as a person or thing having only an imaginary or unverifiable existence.[10] A very famous myth was the Earth was flat. Pythagoras first postulated it was round sometime around 500 BC, yet it was a matter of speculation into the 3rd century BC. The myth began to be challenged when Hellenistic astronomers quantified the spherical shape by calculating the Earth's circumference. It wasn't until the Late Antiquity and Middle Ages that the paradigm was adopted. Again, we can prove or disprove a myth.

---

[10] https://www.merriam-webster.com/dictionary/myth

Legend, by definition, is a combination of both rumor and myth—a story coming down from the past, *especially* one popularly regarded as historical although not verifiable.[11] One of the most famous legends of all was King Arthur and the Knights of the Round Table. We can neither prove nor disprove this. Who's to say that the legend was based on an idea from a true King?

Christ could be considered all three of the above. There is a Christ myth theory where Earl Dougherty[12] argues for a version of the Christ myth theory, the thesis that Jesus did not exist as a historical figure. Doherty says that Paul thought of Jesus as a spiritual being executed in a spiritual realm.[13] And yet according to a 2011 Pew Research Center survey, there were 2.19 billion Christians around the world who believe otherwise. The numbers alone would imply that Dougherty is incorrect in his assumptions, so what do we believe?

Perhaps the answer comes more in it isn't so much what we believe but in how we apply our beliefs. We

---

[11] https://www.merriam-webster.com/dictionary/legend
[12] Earl J. Doherty (born 1941) is a Canadian author of *The Jesus Puzzle* (1999), *Challenging the Verdict* (2001), and *Jesus: Neither God Nor Man* (2009).
[13] Dougherty, Earl, The Jesus Puzzle; Canadian Humanist Publications (1737); Ottawa, Ontario, Canada; January 1999.

use religion, science, what we believe to justify our knowledge, yet our knowledge can be used for good or bad. I have seen those who use religion to justify their acts. To judge, persecute, and worse. I have seen those use proven facts to justify their acts. The murder whose lawyer uses faulty genetics as a defense. I have seen those use the disbelief of God to justify their acts. There is no God, therefore, there are no spiritual consequences in my actions. It comes down to basics—what do we do with what we believe. On this note, I leave you with the following quote to ponder:

> *"People live their lives bound by what they accept as correct and true. That's how they define "reality." But what does it mean to be "correct" or "true"? Merely vague concepts... Their "reality" may all be a mirage. Can we consider them to simply be living in their own world, shaped by their beliefs?"*
>
> *-   Itachi Uchiha (Masashi Kishimoto)*

Chapter 2

Societal Interpretations

"Real eyes, Realize, Real lies."

- *Tupac*

Define Perceptions and Realities

Perceptions and realities are different for each person. But are perceptions and realities the same? Are the terms synonymous? A perception, in terms of beliefs, is a thought, belief, or opinion, often held by many people and based on appearances, whereas reality is the actual state of things or the facts involved in such a state.[14] Clearly, they are not the same. A perception leaves room for interpretation whereas a reality is backed by fact. However, if a person's perception is skewed, then their reality is definitely affected. What determines our realities?

---

[14] https://dictionary.cambridge.org/us/dictionary/english

Focus can determine reality. Some of us are easily swayed by what we see and hear. In this case, our wisdom gives us the option to choose. It isn't something with a right or wrong—barring the obvious—it's a matter of the focus in the moment.

Colin Kaepernick believed in kneeling during the national anthem (also known as tebowing after Tim Tebow, an NFL player who knelt after each pass he threw) because he wanted to bring attention to his perception of systematic racism in America. Does his perception skew the reality? Sadly, no. Racism still exists in our society and is easily substantiated by facts. Many believe that he chose the wrong platform to voice, or in this case, make his point, while as many others believe there wasn't anything 'wrong' in what he did.

> "Just because you're correct doesn't mean you're right."
>
> *Shirou (Kinoko Nasu)*

In a case like this, I believe there is no right or wrong. What he did came from the conviction of his beliefs. He used his high visibility to make a point in a peaceful, unobtrusive way. I have acquaintances who disagree with me, and that's ok too. What I perceive as right may be wrong to someone else. My beliefs come from a different perspective than those who disagree with me.

We all want to be right, though. Egos take over, and objectivity is lost. We don't want our ideas to be wrong or false. For some, being proven wrong is very traumatic. These differences, however, do perpetuate divisiveness. After the over-the-top anti-kneeling media campaign, it then became somewhat of a fad to kneel for everything from our religious beliefs, political beliefs, to our favorite pizza. The good that came of that was that it brought many things to the attention of the public.

This is one of many incidents that encouraged me to develop the convictions of my beliefs. In turn, I encourage you to believe in what you want, despite what people say. The easy route to not challenge allows for complacency to set in. Everything is ok, so just go with it. That's the same as not going to the doctor because you're afraid they're going to find something wrong. If there is something wrong, it is infinitely easier to treat than if we wait. By the same token, if we don't evaluate and challenge our beliefs, we don't evolve. Live your life and go with what you feel is right and not by what someone else has told you. Don't allow yourself to be brainwashed. If you feel differently speak-up, it's ok.

Live a life you believe and not one that is contrived. This universe is continually working to give you what it thinks you want most. Our job is to decide what is right for us. No one else can do that for us. We are each unique in our circumstances and experience, and these things define our beliefs, hence, who we are.

Chapter 3

Mark of the Chosen

"If a fish lives its whole life in this river, does he know the river's destiny? No! Only that it runs on and on out of his control. He may follow where it flows, but he cannot see the end."

- *Jeong Jeong (Bryan Konietzko and Michael Dante DiMartino)*

Fated Passageway

I wonder if we can create our destiny or if what we create is our destiny? Finding the path to our destiny is a quest that humans have been on since the dawn of man. But what is "destiny" exactly? To understand that, we need to look at the history of what determines destiny.

Early on, destiny was perceived as the fate of individual mortals versus the universal abstract of necessity. This meant everyone had his or her own fate. According to 6th Century BCE Greek Philosopher Heraclitus, "...everything depended on destiny, and destiny meant necessity. The essence of destiny was reason, which guided everything."[15] Taking it further, necessity was broken down into fatal sources like oracles, sorceresses, magicians, and anything perceived to control fate or destiny.

The premise of fatalism is the assumption that our lives are predetermined by either supernatural or natural forces—depending on what you believe—which in turn implies that we are not responsible for what happens. Conversely, popular western belief is that we are in control of our destiny, and everything that happens to us is a result of our choices.

Given this philosophical contradiction, what is destiny, and how do we set on the path? Miriam and Webster define destiny as *'a predetermined course of events often held to be an irresistible power or agency.'* Well, here we are again, where we go is predetermined. Perhaps then the question is not so much what is our destiny, but what is the path to our destiny? The road we choose and the decisions we make along the way will determine our journey.

The path to our destiny is influenced at the level of body, mind, heart, and spirit, and therefore, are

---

[15] Spirkin, Alexander; Dialectical Materialism; Progress Publishers, 1987; Moscow, Germany

linked to external or historic influences already built into our matrix. For example, if I was blinded in an accident, my choices would be different then if I were sighted. I would have to learn to navigate the world again through different cues. Perhaps my original plan was to become a pilot. Clearly, a pilot must have sight, so my path has changed. Another example of cause and effect, in terms of destiny, would be making a bad decision like robbing a bank or abusing a spouse. These decisions change our path.

Our journey nurtures us into who we will ultimately be. There will be many bifurcations on our path that we'll have to choose from on the journey to our destiny. What is important to remember is that you choose to move forward and not become complacent. In the grand scheme of time, we are on this earth for a very short period. It is what we do in this time that is so critical to who we are. We will make mistakes along the way, we're only human, but that doesn't mean we can't "fix it." It's perfectly fine to close doors and open new ones. It is the only way to find the path. Even if you walk through the "wrong door," you can turn around. Much like Rome wasn't built in a day, we can't change our destiny overnight. It takes work and commitment as well as a degree of flexibility. Sometimes we have to start over, and that can be daunting, particularly the older we get. It is absolutely still possible if you persevere.

Foundation

In chapter 1 we discussed what life is, beliefs and foundation. Foundation remains critical in choosing paths as well. It is the base or stronghold of our structure. Foundations can be moral or spiritual.

Moral foundation has five basic premises according to Foundational Theory.

- **Care/Harm** - we have the ability to care become attached to others as well as feel and empathize.
    - kindness
    - gentleness
    - nurturance
- **Fairness/Cheating** - we value those who reciprocate our kindness giving us a sense of:
    - justice
    - rights
    - autonomy
- **Loyalty/Betrayal** – we form bonds with people who are like minded developing:
    - devotion
    - self-sacrifice for the friend or group
- **Authority/Subversion** – Humans form hierarchical social interactions developing:
    - leadership

- followership
- deference to authority
- respect for traditions
- **Sanctity/Degradation** – This foundation is based on the psychology of disgust and contamination. It helps to develop:
  - strive to live in a more noble, less carnal way
  - the body is a temple that can be desecrated by acts of immorality and contaminants (drugs, alcohol, etc.)[16]

Given these five basic premises, we can see how they will help to determine the path we choose and what the opposite effects would be. For example, looking at Sanctity – if we consume large amounts of alcohol or other brain altering substances, our ability to make a sound decision is impaired and the path we choose would more than likely be disastrous.

A spiritual foundation is more difficult to define. We must first start by defining what spirituality means to us. The Buddhist definition is *shamatha*, or tranquil abiding, to others it means the spirit aspect of who we are, and still others believe it is their

---

[16] Graham, Jess et al; Moral Foundations Theory: The Pragmatic Validity of Moral Pluralism; November 2012; https://s3.amazonaws.com/academia.edu.documents

connection to something greater than themselves—a higher power. For our purposes, we'll use the following definition:

Spirituality is not about religion. Rather it is an acknowledgement of our spiritual essence by exploring our desire for purpose, meaning and an interconnection with others.

When we consider the definitions of spiritual and moral foundation, we see that without employing one or both philosophies, we cannot withstand the storms of life we may be facing—whether they are financial, emotional, or relational.

Our foundations help us to stay strong by giving us something to draw from. It can be acceptance of the situation, recognition of a belief system, or even a promise we've made to ourselves. Whatever your foundation is, be sure that it is something that will see you through life's difficult moments. For example, perhaps you've lost your job or have been cut from a team that you really love. Your foundation will boost your spirit and keep you going, preventing you from falling into despair.

Ultimately, we choose our paths, and while there are poor choices, there are no wrong answers. It's what we do with the lessons we learn along the way that make the difference.

Chapter 4

What Steers You?

"You have brains in your head. You have feet in your shoes. You can steer yourself any direction you choose"

– *Dr. Seuss*

Onslaught from the Core

Everything we do is based on an attempt to meet core human needs. Maslow identified 5 basic human needs.

- physiological
- safety
- love/belonging
- esteem
- self-actualization

Physiological needs are the first steps to human motivation. These include:

- Homeostasis
- Food
- Water
- Sleep
- Clothes

- Shelter
- Sex

If we are struggling to meet our basic physiological needs, then we are unlikely to pursue our other human needs.

Safety is our second greatest need once the physiological needs have been achieved. Safety and Security needs include:

- Personal security
- Emotional security
- Financial security
- Health and well-being
- Safety needs against accidents/illness and their adverse impacts

These needs can manifest themselves as job security, health and/or car insurance, taking martial arts or self-defense classes, virtually anything that will make us feel safer. If we don't feel safe, again, we won't seek the next level of need.

Love/belonging is third in Maslow's hierarchy and very strong during childhood. In fact, sometimes, it overrides the first two needs, as evidenced by a child who seeks out the abusive parent. Love/belonging are social needs which include:

- Friendships
- Intimacy

- Family

Humans need to be loved, both emotionally and physically. Without it, loneliness and depression can set in.

The fourth need, Esteem, addresses our ego and status. We develop a need for recognition, importance, status, as well as respect from others. This represents the human need to be accepted and respected, which directly affects our self-esteem. Again, with low self-esteem, depression can set in distracting from seeking other needs either higher or lower in the hierarchy.

The final need is Self-Actualization. This is the realization of our full potential.

As humans, we very specifically focus on this need. Some may have a strong desire to be an ideal parent, a star athlete, to paint, or become a renowned scientist. Maslow believed that in order to achieve this level, we first must not only achieve the previous levels but master them.

"Power comes in response to a need, not a desire. You have to create that need"

- *Goku (Akira Toriyama)*

Understanding Maslow's Hierarchy of Needs helps to look at why we do the things we do. We are trying to achieve a specific need. An example would be someone who focuses their energy on material things like the best car, house, or the best clothes. While this may work for them, it may not work for the person who focuses their energy on helping others in need. How did they come to be at polar opposites of their life's desires? It goes back to everything we've discussed so far; beliefs, foundation, paths, and life experience.

Motivation

What is perhaps most important to evaluate is what motivates us to make the choices we make. Motivation is defined as the reason for our actions, willingness, and goals. It is derived from the English language word motivate, which means a desire that needs to be satisfied. Motives are as individual as the person making a choice.

The person who chooses materialism may be motivated by the desire to provide the best for their family, where keeping up appearances was never part of the equation. By the same token, another may have been motivated by a need to perceive themselves better than anyone else. These needs can be desires that were acquired through a variety of influences, including culture, society, or even generally innate.

Intention

Our intentions play an important role in the outcome of the decisions we make along our journey. Intention is defined as a determination to act a certain way. It can also be considered the starting point of every dream or desire, whether it's a relationship, money, or a spiritual awakening. Everything that happens in our lives begins with intention.

Motivation and intention are often used synonymously; however, they are not. We are motivated to carry out our intentions. As such, it is wise to question and understand our intentions. An example would be my intent to become an engineer. Originally the intent was motivated by money—I wanted to be financially successful. As time progressed, the workload became more taxing, and the courses more difficult. At this point, money was no longer the motivation, but intent was to complete my coursework. I had to take a step back and re-evaluate my motivation. In my case, I didn't want to spend the rest of my life thinking I couldn't do it. My motivation changed from money to proving to myself that I could earn my engineering degree regardless of the hardships placed in front of me.

Our motives/reasons and intentions do make a difference in the outcome. Don't be afraid to re-evaluate your reasons if the road changes. Your circumstances in the moment may seem insurmountable, but don't forget to look around. See the single mother struggling to feed her children, the child whose parents are drug addicts, or the soldier who lost a limb fighting for our country. Remember, the paths to our destinies is hardly ever straight forward, and certainly not without trials and tribulations. Embrace them; it's what will make you who you are meant to be.

Hoodwinked Beauty

Physical beauty is an inherited trait, while inner beauty comes from the inside and is something that can be achieved. Physical beauty is appearance, complexion, and physical features. Inner beauty includes characteristics, traits, and personality. Inner beauty is reflected out while physical is how you appear to other people. The idea is to focus on inner beauty and not obsess over your looks.

Physical beauty matters, but you need more than that to attract "real" people into your life. If you judge someone by their physical beauty, it's the same as only looking at the cover of a book. Your inner beauty is what matters. Of course, you need to take pride in yourself and dress nicely, be well-groomed, but the same care is needed for inner beauty. Inner beauty contributes the most in practical life.

Practicality, in this sense, means that it is the person you are that matters. Your inner traits are what make you unique. They are your personality, and that is something that no one can duplicate. They can wear the same clothes, drive the same car, have the same hairstyle, but they will not have the same personality. The purity inside of you glows on the outside; this will attract honest, real people.

What's inside our hearts defines us. What's the point in being pretty on the outside when you are ugly on the inside? If the whole world was blind, how many people would you impress? Even the shiniest wrapping paper sometimes conceals the most disappointing present. It's always what's inside that truly counts. People who are attracted to you because of a pretty face or nice body won't be by your side forever. But the people who can see how beautiful your heart is will never leave you.

> *"Imperfection is beauty, madness is genius and it's better to be absolutely ridiculous than absolutely boring"*
>
> *- Marilyn Monroe*

If you feel you're not the prettiest in the room or maybe not the one that others seek out first, then don't feel bad or jealous of those that do have those things going for them. A pretty soul is far more attractive than soulless beauty. A person who looks great but doesn't do great for others is an ugly person inside. If you don't feel beautiful on the outside, then be beautiful inside.

If all women wore no makeup and comfortable clothes, guys would have no choice but to fall for girls because of the natural beauty. Makeup doesn't make you prettier. Money doesn't make you richer. Real wealth and real beauty depend on how you value yourself. Throw away your mask and put on your soul for a change. Makeup should never be used to hide, it should be used to enhance and improve yourself, not your insecurities. Beauty doesn't rinse off. Outer beauty attracts but inner beauty captivates. Women wear makeup because of a few simple things. It makes them feel beautiful, gives them confidence, helps them be more empowered, and makes them more attractive. But don't get me wrong, no amount of makeup can make you happy unless you choose to be happy from your heart. A pretty face gets old, a nice body will change, but a good person will always be good.

Opinions of Others

"Do you always want to live hiding behind the mask you put up for the sake of others? You're you, and there's nothing wrong with that"

- *Ymir (Hajime Isayama)*

We can spend our whole life trying to be what others want us to be, but what is it that you want to be? We want to control everything. but why? We desire specific things, but why? The answer is the opinions of others. We care about what others will say, so we live in a way they can't express their opinion. We wish to control everything because if we can control everything, then we can control what others can see or say. We yearn for specific things because we will know how others will perceive us. Caring about the opinions of others can lead you down a path unknown to who you see in the mirror.

Many of us worry too much about what others think of us. We overestimate how much and badly others think about our feelings. Consequently, we are far more inhibited and less spontaneous than we could be. Studies conducted by Stavisky et al,[17] showed that common fears associated with worrying about what others think were exaggerated. On a good note, this is something we recognize and therefore, can overcome.

Professor Raj Raghunathan with the McCombs School of Business at The University of Texas at Austin offers these three principles to stop being bothered by what other people think:

- Operate from other-centeredness
    - One way to break this vicious cycle is to operate from a place of *other-centeredness*, rather than self-centeredness. If you are consistently kind and considerate, then you will worry less about what others think of you. There are two reasons why. First, others will naturally like you more when

---

[17] Savitsky, K., Epley, N., & Gilovich, T. (2001). Do others judge us as harshly as we think? Overestimating the impact of our failures, shortcomings, and mishaps. *Journal of Personality and Social Psychology, 81*(1), 44-56. http://dx.doi.org/10.1037/0022-3514.81.1.44

you are kind and considerate; so, you won't need to worry as much about what others think of you.
- Recognize that hurt people hurt people
    - Hurt people *do* hurt people. Even if you do your best to be kind and considerate, you may still be judged negatively by others. This is not a reflection of your failings; rather, it is a reflection on where others are coming from.
- Develop attentional control
    - Sometimes, you may realize that others' negative judgments of you are justified: you simply screwed up. But that doesn't mean that you have to wallow in embarrassment and shame forever. [18]

"It is our choices...that show what we truly are, far more than our abilities."

- *J.K. Rowling*

The truth is, we care so much about what other people think of us, it prevents us from being who we are. This affects everything from what we wear to what we order in a restaurant. We've all done it; it's part of being human. Getting hung up with it is the

---

[18] https://www.psychologytoday.com/us/blog/sapient-nature/201603/how-not-worry-about-what-others-think-you

downfall. I can go on and on about the why's and the don'ts, but personal trainer Nia Shanks summarizes it perfectly in the following 10 steps.

1. **This is the most obvious benefit: life is better when you're not so concerned about how other people will view you for your actions, choices, and decisions.** There's great freedom from doing what makes you happy; being authentically yourself.

2. **We're overly concerned with what others think of us, and don't even realize it.** Once you stop basing your choices off of what you expect other people to think, or how they might react, you'll notice that many do what you used to: make choices based on the concern of others' opinions.

3. **Many people don't care nearly as much as we think they will.** If you are overly concerned with how you dress, then you wear what you think other people expect you to wear. What you may not realize is that *they don't give a darn.* Many times, we expect people to have a greater opinion over our choices than they do, likely because they're concerned with their own

lives and choices (and may be overly concerned with what *you* think about *their* choices!).

4. **People like you more.** When you don't base your life choices on what you assume other people might think, people are free to see *the real you.* This authenticity—raw beauty stripped of the facade—is illuminating. Those who already like you will begin to appreciate you even more.

5. **People who didn't like you in the first place still won't like you.** You may not see this as a benefit. Think of it this way, if someone didn't like you when you were trying to be what they wanted or expected, they may still not like you once you stop caring what they think. This is a good thing. Not everyone will like you; let these people fall to the wayside. You don't need them in your life.

6. **You establish a clear idea of what you want to accomplish.** Once you stop caring about others' opinions, your personal goals and desires became much clearer. Now you are free to pursue your passions without the burden of wondering *what they will think of me* and adjusting your course.

7. **Some people just aren't nice.** Some people will always judge you. Some will always gossip about you. Whether you do what they think is right or do what you want, they will always be there to criticize your every decision. These same individuals likely don't follow The One Rule to Not Suck at Life, so they're allowing their true character to shine forth.

8. **You experience less stress.** Trying to be something you're not is exhausting. Dictating your choices on the assumed thoughts of others is suffocating. When you are yourself, this stress melts away. You may not realize how much unnecessary stress you're experiencing from being concerned with what other people think of you until you quit doing so. Life is stressful enough; let's not increase it by being overly concerned with what other people think.

9. **Integrity abounds. What you do is in line with your values.** I respect others who hold true to their values (even if they're different than mine) more than those who bend at the whim of society or other people.

10. **Growth becomes easier and enjoyable.** With each passing year, life experiences increase, and you get a bit smarter. This accumulating experience and knowledge, coupled with actively living your life and not allowing the assumed thoughts of others control you, will allow you to grow as a human.[19]

"If nobody cares to accept you and wants you in this world, accept yourself and you will see that you don't need them and their selfish ideas."

- Alibaba Saluja

In summary, be who you want to be? Stop living with pain in order to not be judged. Stop worrying about how others think of you. I can't express this enough. Of course, care about the way you give off, but be yourself. Celebrities do all kinds of crazy stuff, but yet it's considered "cool" as opposed to a regular person doing it; then they look "funny." Perceptions come and go, which is why you should do what you want and be your own person. Be so comfortable that if people are mean to you, it doesn't faze you one bit. Have the mental toughness to release your energy only when due.

---

[19] https://www.niashanks.com/one-rule-not-suck-life/

Do what your heart desires, never hold back a thing, and don't worry so much about what others think, because at the end of the day, what makes you happy is what really matters. Besides, how can someone truly love you if you aren't being you? You are a beautiful thing.

Chapter 5

Dream Unimaginably

"They've promised that dreams can come true but forgot to mention that nightmares are dreams, too"

- Oscar Wilde

Vivid Dreams

Dreams are stories and images, but they are also thoughts, sounds and voices, and subjective sensations. They can include people and places we know and those we don't or have never been. Dreams can be about what happened that day, your deepest fears, or even your desires.

We have dreams of who we want to be, things we'd like to have, and goals we'd like to achieve. Can they be interchangeable? Yes, in that perhaps you've dreamt of achieving your goal. However, these dreams are cognitive in our awake state. (Not to be confused with the state of cognitive dreaming). Think of this dream as a vision that motivates us to make our goals a reality. From the education we complete to the cars we drive, dreamers can manifest what they want most in life. This is why dreams are so important.

Every great achievement begins with a dream. So, what's the secret to making our dreams come true? How do we know if we are being realistic? To address this, let's look at Walt Disney. He had a dream—Disneyland. Mr. Disney had a dream to build this amusement park in 1950. He saw his dream open to the public on July 15, 1955. Can you imagine the number of people who laughed at the concept of his dream back then? It wasn't a reality... until it was. He made his dream come true as unreal as it may have seemed. In an interview he was asked what makes dreams come true, he answered, "The secret of making dreams come true can be summarized in four C's. They are Curiosity, Confidence, Courage, and Constancy; and the greatest of these is Confidence."

Don't be afraid to dream and to dream big. Take a risk and go big but have a plan and courage to endure the journey no matter what you are up against. There is always a price to pay for the work involved in making dreams come true. It is important though, that you don't lose your happiness in the process. Don't dwell on your dreams so much that you forget to live your own life. Plan but enjoy and appreciate every day.

"Anything you can imagine, you can create."

- Oprah Winfrey

Emma Seppala, Ph.D states, "…if you prioritize your happiness, you will actually be more productive, more creative, more resilient, more energized, more charismatic and influential."[20] Logic will take you from A to B, but imagination and dreams will take you to a place that fills your heart with the same feeling a little kid has when he goes to an amusement park or watches his favorite show at a concert.

What do you envision?

The sky is never the limit; your vision is unless you allow it to be. The choice is yours. You can wake up in the morning and decide to go back to sleep and keep dreaming, or you get up and chase your dream.

Dreams can also change while in the pursuit of making it happen. Things can also go wrong when

---

[20] https://www.psychologytoday.com/us/blog/feeling-it/201610/the-secret-achieving-your-dreams-no-one-tells-you-about

chasing our dreams. If it doesn't happen, it doesn't mean you "failed" it means, "you've found ways that don't work." Stay positive, have faith, and continually show courage. If you don't follow your heart, you may well spend the rest of your life wishing you had.

Commitment is the difference between those who live out their dreams and those that don't. Those who persevere are committed just that badly, they will do anything to see their dream or a dream they believe in come to fruition.

In anime, a majority of the time, the main character has no power but by the end of the story, he is one of the strongest because fulfilling his lifelong dream or goal is what's important to him. I preach that it is not how you start but how you finish.

Future belongs to whom?

There is greatness in all of us. You can be the CEO of your own company if you choose and you believe. There is no timetable for success except for the one you impose upon it. If you believe it's too late, then it is too late. If you believe you can still live out your dreams, then they will come true.

Not placing a specific timetable on a dream is a good strategy to succeed, but not chasing the dream in a reasonable time period is a surety for failure. Many people think they will figure it out as time goes, then bam, 10 years have gone by. While you have to have long terms goals, you also need to set short term goals to get the dream on the track.

Dreams sit on a shelf because we make excuses. We have too many responsibilities; our job is too demanding. Whatever the excuse, we always have time to watch TV or have a beer a couple of nights a week. What if we took that time to work on our dream? All things come with a price. If you really want to see your dreams come to fruition, then you have to sacrifice some of your time. My point is too grind now and ponder later while attacking your aspirations.

Dreams are a funny thing. In the course of our lifetimes, we have multiple dreams inspired by our experience in life. Something we dreamt at 15, we may laugh about at 30 and something at 30, we'll laugh at in our 60's. One of my favorite quotes is by Eleanor Roosevelt: "The future belongs to those who believe in the beauty of their dreams."

Patience

We move at our own pace in life, do not feel like you are behind because you don't move at "society's" pace. Like go to college right after high school or getting married by 30. Those are life's standards, and you have your own life—live it. Stand up and fight for your dreams, have the conviction to succeed. When we are patient, we'll have a greater appreciation for success.

Your dream isn't going to happen overnight. You have to go step by step and be ready to change the course many times over. When you do achieve your goal, be sure it makes you happy. Sometimes what we think will make us happy doesn't until we are actually experiencing it. That's ok too. Look at Elan Musk. His dream was to send ships to space and eventually, space travel. Is that where the dream started? Did you know he started as an engineer with a software company that eventually became PayPal, which sold to eBay for $1.5 billion? He had and has many other endeavors, now including SpaceX, which successfully launched the first private company designed/built rocket into space. His dream came true, but it didn't happen overnight.

How do we decide what our dreams or goals should be? It goes back to what I mentioned earlier in the book; what motivated your dream or goal. If the motivation was to seek revenge or has malicious intent, then that isn't worth pursuing. Our dreams and goals should make us happy first and foremost. And, if it doesn't pan out, don't jump blindly into something else. Take a step back and re-evaluate. Create a new blueprint then attack. Sometimes dreams that don't pan out are meant to teach lessons. These lessons and people you meet are great additions to your life.

Remember, if you do what you have always done, then how do you expect to get different results? Never be afraid to try something new because repetition can become boring, especially when you stay within the limits of what you already know. It's better to look back on life and say, "I can't believe I did that," rather than say, "I wish I had done that." Not all things you try will work out, but somethings will. Keep figuring yourself out like trial and error, but understand what the error is before you decide to give up on one thing and try another. Also, try new things to see what may excite you as sometimes we don't know how much fun we would have until we're actually playing the game. Like watching a movie, you thought you didn't like based on the cover and description, yet after watching it, it becomes one of your top movies.

Vow to my Goals

"What you get by achieving your goals is not as important as what you become by achieving your goals."

– *Henry David Thoreau*

Remember that goals are good for setting a direction toward your path. You will run into doubt, fear, exhaustion, and yearning, but that is what makes chasing a goal so thrilling, the high you feel from overcoming all is like no other.

Goals don't have to be gigantic; they can be minuscule, yet that minuscule goal can branch into bigger goals. You can have a goal to clean out the garage or revamp your room; it doesn't have to be just about attaining riches. Use goals to change, not define. Our goals can breed a structure that we can live by, which is the purpose, not just to acquire a specific accolade. We can regress once that goal is completed like a women's Vegas trip, so staying true to yourself and the structure you develop is what matters. Life is a goal itself, so live a way where you produce time and time again like how top colleges keep getting the best recruits and winning championships. Obviously, the goal is to win a championship, but developing that winning structure is what is prudent to tackling that endeavor.

Rejoice in the mini-milestones; I can't express this enough. A lot of people become consumed by achievement which can inadvertently create a negative effect including loneliness. The thought of once I attain this or achieve this, that my life will change can keep you on a continual goal treadmill. Don't kill yourself or happiness with the thought of bringing your dreams to fruition, as stated by Emma Seppala earlier in the chapter. Have the belief and faith that, with hard work, what's best for you will manifest itself when the time is right. You may realize that the journey towards the goal was actually better than achieving it.

Life is sometimes like a GoPro camera—focus on what's important, and you'll capture it perfectly. If it is important to you, you will find a way. If not, you'll find an excuse. Before you tackle these goals, vow to yourself that you will accomplish these no matter what, as this will start a great streak for your future. Concentrate on what is important and commit to it all the way. Don't do things half-ass because you are scared of failure. Remember, failure is necessary for you to grow. Commit with your heart and soul and work like no other and watch what happens to not only your mindset but your life. Ask yourself what is important to you? What do I not want taken away from me? What can't I live without?

For your first mission, I challenge you to complete 5 goals by the end of next year and write down 5 goals you want to accomplish by the end of your lifetime. See if any of these answers change when you are finished reading. Embrace the journey, and never lose sight of the finish line.

Part II

Awakening

X

Acknowledgement

Chapter 6

Lost Connections

"One of the lessons that I grew up with was to always stay true to yourself and never let what somebody says distract you from your goals."

- Michelle Obama

Childhood

When you're a kid, and somebody asks what you want to be when you grow up, your answer is limitless. As you get older, that answer becomes far more streamlined. Why do you think that is? There are multiple answers to  this. The first of which may be that when we are young, we are like sponges and absorb everything. One week we may study dinosaurs and want to be a paleontologist, the next week the teacher may have done a cool experiment in class and made a volcano erupt, so now we want to be a chemist. We are excited and stimulated by every possibility.

In our teenage years, our influences change. Perhaps we are inspired by a race car driver, a boxer, a rock star, or an actor. In these cases, you might hear the usual rant that the economy is worse than ever, and how are you going to make a living doing that, or, "do you know how many actors there are waiting on tables?" So, we learn to tailor our answers to avoid the lectures. But it could also be that maybe we don't understand the grind that comes with the careers we choose and after a bit of research, we decide that's not what we want to sign up for. And all of that is ok. However, it's ok to dream and dream big. If one dream doesn't happen, there's another waiting in the wings. Don't let that child get lost in the rants of others or your fear.

"You're never too old to be young."

- Snow White (Grimm Brothers)

Not everything comes easy in life, and sometimes what we think we want doesn't happen. When I was a kid, I wanted to be in the NBA—now I just want to impact people's lives. When you are a kid, you have so many dreams, and those dreams change. Change is part of life, so if one thing doesn't work out, then find something that will. Don't give up. Even when things seem pointless, continue to persevere. It took me years to see my grind pay off, but it all happened at the right time. The trials and tribulations I overcame made me a stronger person. I look back in on how I was able to keep going and am proud I didn't give up.

Imagine going into the future and telling you, "Aye, I'm going to give up." How do you think your future self will react? Why should you want to keep going when something is painful or stressful? A study published in the *Journal of Leadership and Organizational Studies* showed that being able to push through tough times is linked to greater success in the present as well as future. So, don't give up. Keep going when you fall. Get up even if you fall again. Think of what would have happened if Edison had given up after the first time the lightbulb didn't work? He was asked by a reporter how he felt about failing 1,000 times, and Edison responded, "I have not failed. I just found 1000 ways that will not work." Like Edison, don't let things in life stop you from growing and becoming the best version of yourself.

Be true to your own dream. It's easy to see something that someone else has and want that. Some would say being a celebrity is the best lifestyle, but then why do some commit suicide? No matter who or what, we are all human and subject to a gamut of human emotions. Pursuing your dream should make you happy. J Cole once said happiness is the highest level of success.

The funny thing is when we're kids; we think we know so much. The reality is we know very little. It's a time in our lives where we should be carefree. We don't have to pay bills; we don't have to work. Our biggest responsibility, for most of us, is to grow and learn. For those who have experienced horrible things, there are studies that now show it can make them stronger. Studies of resilience show that exposure to early challenges that don't destroy us may actually enhance our ability to cope with future threats.[21] Again, not the way any child should grow up, but there is hope.

Whether our upbringing was storybook perfect or tumultuous, one thing we all tend to do as we grow

---

[21] https://www.psychologytoday.com/us/blog/nurturing-resilience/201603/horrible-true-early-abuse-can-create-strength

older is loose our child. As children, we are eager to become adults, and once we get here, stress can make us want to go back to childhood. Of course, we can't turn back the hands of time. But there are childlike characteristics that we can hold onto to live a better life.

> **Curiosity** - Curiosity opens doors mentally, breeds creativity, and spurs imagination.
> **Excitement** - Use the perspective of a child to re-ignite the passion for life you once possessed
> **Faith** - Develop the faith of a child and use it to take the leaps necessary to live a successful and rewarding life
> **Trust** - As human beings we need others in our lives to be fulfilled, so let your guard down a little bit and allow people to have a place in your heart and in your life, it'll make you a happy person.
> **Wonder** - The world is a pretty cool place when you take the time to observe it with wonder.
> **Short memory** - Life is way too short to let past pains, betrayals, and disappointments linger and marinate in our minds.

> **Persistence** - Develop the persistence of a child when attempting to tackle your goals and ambitions. Don't give up until you get what you want.[22]

"A child can teach an adult three things: to be happy for no reason, to always be busy with something, and to know how to demand with all his might that which he desires."

- Paulo Cahello

When we are children, we seldom think of the future. This innocence leaves us free to enjoy ourselves as few adults can. The day we fret about the future is the day we leave our childhood behind. Now the keyword is fret. Be wise and plan for a future where you envision happy, but don't lose that innocence inside of you. Flow with life, and do not fret about things that are out of your control.

Old Wounds

Have you ever wondered why some Disney movies still have meaning to us to this day? We love our childhood movies because the characters remind us of ourselves when we were growing up, whether the experience was good or bad.

---

[22] https://thoughtcatalog.com/ayodeji-awosika/2015/07/7-childlike-traits-we-should-recapture-to-live-a-happier-life/

The events of our childhood form who we become as adults. Just how and how much those events influence us is a question researchers are still trying to answer. A study done in the late 90s by Kaiser-Permanente and the CDC found that adverse childhood experiences were suffered by more than 30% of their subjects. That's a high percentage. The study also showed the following:

- Substance abuse in household   28.2%
- Physical abuse   26.4%
- Parental separation or divorce   24.1%
- Sexual abuse   21%
- Mental illness in household   20.3%
- Emotional neglect   14.8%
- Battered mother   13%
- Emotional abuse   10.2%
- Physical neglect   9.9%
- Incarcerated household member   6%

The study also showed that adverse childhood experiences (ACE) very seldom occurred in single events, as shown in the graph below. Specifically, 32.7% of subjects in the study reported 0 incidences of recurrence, 25.6% reported 1 incidence of recurrence, and so on.

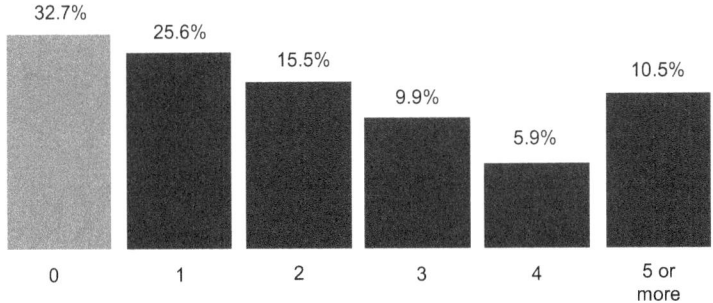

Figure 1 ACE Events Occurrence

Many people grow up and repeat the patterns of abuse they were subjected to as children. *The poem Children Learn What They Live*, written in 1954 by Dorothy Law Nolte, teaches us exactly that. It is a pattern that is very difficult. It's comfortable; it's what is known. In spite of the heinous nature of the abuse, we must find a way to break the cycle. We need to be aware of our own footprint. How do we treat people around us? How do we treat our children? What are we teaching our children in our own behaviors? How are our children living their lives?

> *"Even the most ignorant, innocent child will eventually grow up as they learn what true pain is. It affects what they say, what they think... and they become real people."*
>
> – *Nagato (Masashi Kishimoto)*

Teaching children isn't easy. Kids are curious and anxious to become their own person. Some will follow in your footsteps, and some may be the complete opposite. Like adults, they want to do what makes them happy. We need to listen to what they are saying and find a way to teach without insisting on it being our way. We need to teach them to make responsible choices that have positive effects on their lives as well as the lives they touch. We don't want them to make the same mistakes we did, but we need to let them have some choices. You can't make the same mistake twice because the second time it is a choice. We need to be honest with them and not be deceitful. Granted, there are things children don't need to know at a young age, but as adults, we must accept our past "sins." We need to show that we have moved on, grown beyond whatever the behavior was and that it no longer bothers us. This is the best example we can set for children; we are not perfect, we've made our mistakes, but we've addressed them, fixed them, and have moved on.

Shadow of the Past

Our fears and a lot of our problems are a manifestation of what has happened in our lives and the choices we make as we continue to move through our journey. We gravitate toward the majority and allow our pasts to dictate our present actions. It's true we must learn from our past experiences, but that doesn't mean to become a victim or wallow in self-pity. We need to be able to let go of the anger to move on. We need to be able to overcome our fears before they fester in problems. The moment you realize that your problems are your own is the moment you truly grow.

We try to live with our problems as it is perceived as being strong. In reality, it's just a weight vest as yes, it will make you strong, but to wear it 24/7 is detrimental in the grand scheme of things. It is cool to be strong, but when you're strong, nobody asks if you are okay.

> *"You're not defined by your past; you're prepared by it. You're stronger, more experienced, and you have greater confidence."*
>
> *– Joel Osteen*

So many people in this world dwell on the past. We cannot change the events of the past. We can beat ourselves up about past mistakes or learn the lessons from the mistakes and move on to the future. A lot of guys miss out on making the pros or getting that scholarship they dreamed of getting and beat themselves up wondering why. They search for something to fill that void but sometimes replace it with the wrong things. What they are placing in the void is only for their pride or ego and not themselves. Our past doesn't define who we are but does affect how we move forward. When we learn and move on, we can create a different identity for ourselves with hard work and determination.

It is also good to remember that there are those who have had more issues to overcome than you or me. Think about the people who have to move from school to school, those who are bullied every day for no reason, those who have no friends—life is not easy for them, but they like you, are not alone. It's crazy how events that happen in our younger days can cause very negative emotions and responses later in life. As difficult as it may seem, the only way to get beyond this is to face the pain and resolve the emotions. Of course, this is easier said than done.

It's made easier if you live one day at a time and remind yourself each day that you deserve better. Don't waste your precious life on the injuries of the past.

Loneliness/Solitude

Do people check on you, or do you always check on others? You may feel like you lost a friend, but were they a true friend to begin with?

Loneliness and solitude are not synonymous. Loneliness is when we have no friends, whereas solitude is a state of alone and can be a choice. Choice meaning perhaps we need solitude to unwind from a busy day or stressful situation. Loneliness, on the other hand, does not necessarily mean being completely isolated from other people. Someone who is depressed or suffering a deep emotional trauma can often feel alone in a crowded room.

Being alone is more painful than pain itself or getting hurt. We all need something in our life that makes us not  feel alone. We need to feel wanted and happy. Knowing that we aren't alone when we are suffering can bring some sense of joy. Feeling alone when sad or deeply hurt is hell on earth, which I equate with loneliness.

You are not alone; we all suffer at one point in our life, but it is our choice never to give up and keep moving forward. I wonder if life continues to throw battles at us because it is a necessity to bring out the best version of us. Without experiencing trials and tribulations, how would we understand what's good or bad? The bad make us appreciate the good. If we never learn to appreciate the good, then is that really life?

You are not alone. You would be surprised how many people are going through exactly what you are going through. You are not the only human going through a bad time. You can overcome these dark times with faith and patience. Don't lose hope.

You are not alone, there is somebody out there who looks up to you and is watching you all the time.

Friendship and human connection are like the air we breathe and the water we drink; as humans we must have them to survive. Psychologists have found that humans have a basic need for group life and close relationships.[23] When these basic human needs aren't met, it can have a profound effect on us both emotionally and physically.

There are times when we so desperately want that sense of belonging that we will make poor decisions. Some people will join a gang, others, a dangerous cult. In these environments, they will feel at home, which is what the heart yearns for. Others will enter into unhealthy relationships, which only add to the sadness. If we are not happy in our relationships, often depression will set in, now making the loneliness feel worse.

Again, people mix up loneliness and solitude. Solitude is time to yourself you choose to have—a place to recharge our batteries that we all need on occasion. Loneliness is no friends, family, spouse, significant other, or place to belong. Just one person can make somebody not feel lonely. If you can be that person to someone, you will find that you aren't lonely either. Connecting with other people, even if it's only one person, will help the feeling of loneliness disappear, and slowly turn into joy.

---

[23] https://www.psychologytoday.com/us/articles/200307/the-dangers-loneliness

You may see others who are experiencing something you've been through. Help them through the storm. Many good people are lost to loneliness, living an unseen life in the shadows. By helping them, you also help yourself.

Doing Things Alone

A lot of times, people who are in pain, choose to keep it to themselves. Either they want to remain private or feel that no one will understand. The truth is quite the contrary. We never know what others are going through or have gone through. It is only through communicating with each other that we will know. It's ok to talk about your pain. Everyone needs help once in a while, and going through it alone only makes life harder.

Your suffering will want you to be alone because it knows only love can beat it. Loving you or getting love from another person can help you cope with the pain. It hurts, but you are different now. Once you've been through the storm, focus your energy on living in the moment and enjoy good times.

Try and live your life happy, not stressed out or unhappy. Don't be afraid to Be You or to Believe in yourself even when things aren't perfect. Have pride in who you are. Choose people who support you instead of those who don't care and would hurt you. You deserve it!

A Single Friend

Cherish the relationships you share with people. We all long for a friend—one who truly enjoys our company the same way we enjoy theirs. Being alone without parents, siblings, or friends is hell on earth. Be friendly and kind to people; it could change their entire life.

Friends are an important part of your life. They can have a major influence on how you think, feel, and behave.[24] You want to look for friends who are supportive and positive; people who know and value your worth. You don't need a lot of people to be happy, just a few who appreciate you for who you are. You want to avoid negative friends to maintain a healthy and active social life. [25]

Here are some things to look for in quality friends:

---

[24] https://www.psychologytoday.com/blog/what-mentally-strong-people-dont-do/201504/5-reasons-studies-say-you-have-choose-your-friends
[25] see 3

- Emotional support and guidance – good friends support you through whatever you're going through.
- Balance of give and take - You should try to cultivate friendships where there is a balance of give and take, and where you do not feel you are giving or taking more than the other person.[26]
- Bring out the best in you - friends should also encourage you to develop into the best version of yourself you can be.[27]
- Effective Communication - positive communication, where you can share your thoughts and feelings without limits. You should not feel you have to censor yourself or keep quiet about your thoughts around your friends. [28] [29]
- Trust and respect - Good friends will stand up for you and support you in company of strangers and other friends.[30]

There are behaviors that should be avoided as well. Those would include:

---

[26] http://www.uklifecoaching.org/friends.htm
[27] http://www.helpguide.org/articles/relationships/how-to-make-friends.htm
[28] http://www.helpguide.org/articles/relationships/how-to-make-friends.htm
[29] http://greatist.com/live/relationship-advice-how-to-be-a-true-friend
[30] see 6 & 7

- Negative Friends
    o put you down in front of others to make themselves look good
- Friends who use you
    o those who give you no encouragement or support but take from you
- He/she only contacts you if it's for something that will benefit them.
- People who are focused on the negative
    o Negative people can cause stress and put you in a permanent state of negativity. [31]

In life, you will realize there is a role for everyone you meet. Some will test you; some will use you; some will love you, and some will teach you. But the ones who are truly important are the ones who bring out the best in you. They are the rare and amazing people who remind you why it's worth having friends or acquaintances.

We have friends that are in huddles, in meetings, in school, by the beach. Friends can be anywhere. As long as you are yourself, you will find those that need to be in your life and you in theirs.

---

[31] http://greatist.com/live/relationship-advice-how-to-be-a-true-friend

Conglomeration

When connecting with others, you may find something important within the relationship or bond you share with someone. You don't always have to be around people who have something to offer; sometimes, we need to be around people to feel less alone. By someone making us feel less alone, we begin to find importance in this person thus giving us a reason for being here. Some people cut people off entirely because they don't want to get hurt. Not everybody will hurt you. When you're scared, you can miss out on so many things, the thrill of the good, the bad, the love, the sadness, and the memories. What looks better, a tree or a forest? Some would ask who these people are to you. I would say that they are people who I consider my friends or family. Are they going to be in your life in 5 years? I would like for them to be in my life, but who knows what the future holds. Until that time comes, I'll enjoy the relationships. How do they make you a better person? You know I don't always need to gain anything from each relationship, sometimes just the person being there is enough for me as it makes me feel less alone.

Chapter 7

Imprisoned Illusions

"True Freedom means freeing oneself from the dictates of the ego and its accompanying emotions"

– Matthieu Ricard

Seductive Ego

What is an ego anyway? By definition, it is a person's sense of self-esteem or self-importance. From a psychological standpoint, it is the part of the mind that mediates between the conscious and the unconscious and is responsible for reality testing and a sense of personal identity. Freud believed that the human psyche has more than one aspect; specifically, three parts: id, ego, and super-ego.

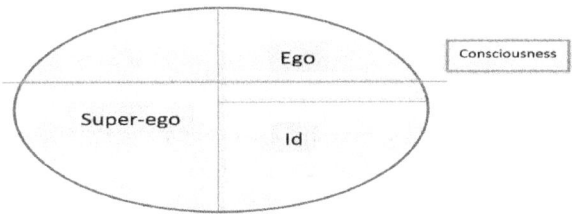

The id is the primitive and instinctual part of the mind that contains sexual and aggressive drives and hidden memories, the super-ego operates as a moral conscience, and the ego is the realistic part that mediates between the desires of the id and the super-ego.[32]

Your ego is how you perceive yourself as well as how you look to others. These perceptions are your sense of self. Your sense of self begins to develop when we are young—about the same time as our id, ego, and super-ego are developing. Our sense of self and therefore, "ego" responses are influenced by family members, friends, clergy, teachers, and the local grocery store clerk.

Sense of self includes roles, attributes, behaviors, and associations we consider most important about ourselves. A strong sense of self is critical, especially today, with so many influences and variables of those influences. A strong sense of self helps us to

---

[32] McLeod, S. A. (2016, Feb 05). *Id, ego and superego.* Retrieved from https://www.simplypsychology.org/psyche.html

deal with conflicts, keep promises we make to ourselves, allows to make our own decisions without seeking counsel every time, allows us to pursue our own interests and not follow the crowd, allows us to set healthy boundaries in terms of what people can ask or expect of us, act authentically and not how "we think" we should act, and know ourselves well enough to decide how true insults are.

While each of these is important, let's focus on the last point; decide how true insults are. Many times, when we choose our own paths, those who don't understand will insult our choices or make fun of us. Our egos need to be well in place, which requires a strong sense of self, but we also need to be able to hear the insult. Is it malicious or was it intended to be constructive? Malicious insults can be discounted. What someone thinks of us doesn't matter because they aren't us. What they may perceive as cool isn't cool to us. Everyone is different.

Having a strong sense of self helps our three egos to work together to form intelligent, strong responses. Understanding the purpose of the ego and how it functions will help us to grow. Typically, when we think of "ego" with think of someone who's self-absorbed, always right, and perhaps feels they are better and smarter than everyone else. While that's true, that's the id part of ego in play where there is no balance with the ego and super-ego. None of us want to be that person, and no one wants to be around that person. Be aware of your reactions and chose your words and actions carefully. Be aware of the choices you make.

Look at people who spend their time chasing rock stars or other celebrities and wanting to hang out with them. Why do you think they want to do this? My opinion is that it enhances their egos. They look cooler, they feel cooler, and they feel more important. This is an illusion. Ultimately, they gain nothing except giving others the false perception that they are important. If you are perceived as something you are not, then whatever someone feels about you cannot be real. How can it be when you are not yourself?

Look at the woman who chases the man with a lot of money. She doesn't care about him; she cares about his wallet. Conversely, he can have any woman he chooses but will usually choose an arm hanger. She may have nothing in common with him, but she looks good. When he's done with her, he'll move on to the next. Why, because it isn't real.

It's all an illusion because ultimately, it does nothing for you except affect how others perceive you. Stop chasing what your ego wants and chase what your heart yearns for. We should live for happiness, not infatuation, or to boost our ego. My point is, be you and stop looking for others to like you for what you have and not what you bring to the table. The ones who support you and who are there for you during the tough times are the real ones. Stop living the life that society wants you to live, live that life you want.

Be yourself and show the world how weird you are. It's funny how rappers wear unique style clothes, yet it's perceived as style. When a "normal" person wears the same thing, they are made fun of. It just goes to show you how much people pay attention to status, so instead of trying to impress, why not try to achieve that status on your own? People will be far more impressed if you've achieved something through hard work and perseverance versus on someone else's coattail.

In reality, the status these guys have they earned. They didn't copy anyone else. Their style is their own. It's ok to be influenced by somebody but don't be them. Be you, and you'll see how much you better you feel. Rejoice when others make fun of you. Try laughing with others when they make fun of you as opposed to getting upset and see what happens. Don't just take it though, have some clever rebuttals too. My point is to have fun and laugh but not to undermine anybody. There's a difference between teasing and belittling someone. Telling somebody their nostrils are as big as the engine of a spaceship as opposed to calling somebody Michael Jackson nose every day. Playful banter is healthy. Belittling someone is not. They don't like it any more than you do.

Something else to think about is if we are right or wrong. It's important to admit that you are wrong. While most people want to be right, it's not always going to happen. Admitting when someone else is right will help you learn and can open doors for you.

Control Your Ego

When you allow your ego to control your thoughts, everything you believe becomes an illusion.[33]

You may think after reading this that having an ego is bad. Well, not quite; having an ego is what differentiates us from others. My message is to

---

[33] Rusty Eric; found on
https://alishbahdiaries.wordpress.com/2017/12/01/aesthetic-selfies-or-self-portraits/

control it, not get rid of it. Understand when it's your ego being hurt as opposed to your heart getting hurt. Other people's opinions don't mean anything in your world, so don't give them any power. When you are comfortable in your own skin, you have become comfortable in your own ego.

Your competition isn't other people. Your competition is your procrastination. Your ego. The unhealthy food you're consuming, the knowledge you neglect. The negative behavior you're nurturing and your lack of creativity. Compete against that.

We can feel so proudly about ourselves when, in reality, nobody even looks at us the way we think others do. Lower your ego. Men, if women think you are attractive, then be humble, don't go around thinking you're this and that. Eventually, your ego will be out of control, and when you feel rejection, it can turn your life upside down. You will search for validation for the ego, which could be bragging about money or even taking someone's girl. Rejoice in the positives in life, don't abuse it. So many times, we take things for granted, and when they are gone, we can slip into depression.

The way to help control your ego is to do something that generates the same high you feel. For example, you may have been "the man" in high school, then when you went to college, that changed. You became a small fish in a big pond. That's a huge blow to the ego because it's used to feeling important and relevant. Now doing something greater can generate that high again, which can help ease the blow the ego suffered. For me, it was being an engineer. Being an engineer made me feel relevant, intelligent, and ambitious, which is how I felt when playing basketball in high school and being "the man."

You must be able to control your ego, not let your selfishness get the best of you. Be humble and thankful for great times, so that when they come to an end, you can smile in awe of the memories and look forward to the next chapter of life.

Happiness or Egotistical Pleasure

Have you ever done something thinking it would make you happy then discovered rather than being happy you were even more at a loss? That was your ego you were satisfying. Look deep within your heart and think about it—is that who you really are? Not to be confused with what others think or want you to be, but what YOU want to be.

We have to continually look for what brings joy to our hearts. Many people lose themselves after high school sports if they don't play college ball. It's all about finding joy within you. Life has so much to offer, and there are things out there that you would love, but your ego or funds won't allow you to do it. Live your own life, get out, explore, and find what makes your heart content.

Most engineers, lawyers, or doctors pick their specific major because they want to make money, yet they realize it's not what they want to do during their final year even though they've come too far to quit. Follow your passion, don't follow the money. Any occupation can make you rich. You could have a janitor service and have people work for you.

Stop feeding your ego. Stop thinking you just look better or are better than everybody else. Stop thinking you're above everybody or people you think aren't cool. We are all too similar to think like this. Look yourself in the mirror and ask, "Am I truly happy? Ask Am I happy where I'm at? Do I find myself constantly arguing?" They say a person who argues a lot has a lot of pain hidden inside.

Do not be afraid to ask for help. I don't know why people are afraid to have others help them when helping one another is the most gratifying thing. Lower your ego and pride because there are people who will know more than you and understand that we all need direction at some point.

We can live life to gratify our egos or live life to help others. When we live life for our ego, a sense of emptiness can form. You do all these things to achieve the things you "want," but when you achieve them, you realize this isn't what you wanted; it was simply your ego. After a while, the feeling will go away, like playing a video game, once you beat it, it just picks up dust, yet there are a few games that make people want to replay them even when they are beaten.

Consumed by the Ego

"Whether we wound or are wounded, the blood that flows is red."

- *Eiichiro Oda*

Remember that we are no better than anybody, no matter what status we've achieved. A CEO of a fortune 500 company still has to eat and sleep the same way as a custodian. They still bleed when they are cut, laugh when they are tickled, and cry when they are hurt. The difference lies more in the power that is acquired. Power is very intoxicating and has consumed many. This can show itself through belittling another person, treating people of lesser status with disrespect, or even callous disregard. No person deserves to be treated inhumanely; we are all humans at the end of the day. Our egos can turn us into people we never wanted to become or thought we could become and it's sad.

Use your ego in a positive way to uplift yourself and others. Use the power that you earned for good and not evil. If you don't know what evil is, then ask yourself, "Would I do this to my mom or kid?" Your ego is like your inside presence. When it is hurt, only you feel the pain, and when it is boosted, only you feel the joy. Your ego can't define you, but you can define it—after all, it is inside of you. It is there to make you different, not an asshole. Embrace your ego, and take pride in it.

When to Use My Ego

Notice a warm-hearted person relaxes and chills. Maybe it's because they understand what's really important in this world and do not worry about little things that don't deserve any attention. They are not likely to engage with the person honking their horn at them, or the person who cuts them off in line. It just doesn't matter to them. They choose their battles carefully.

This isn't to say let others walk over you or take advantage. I'm saying to control your energy and only show emotion when it is needed. If somebody honks at you, should you really get upset? Probably not. Move on with the day. Worry about being the best version of yourself, not the best version of your ego.

Emotions

> *"Healing requires you to feel your emotions, recognize your Ego carries a story and your soul has the capacity to prevail through it all"*
>
> *- Wendy De Rosa*

It's interesting how we hang on to something that we are better off letting go of. It's almost like being an emotional hoarder. We know that there's something better out there, yet we still hang onto whatever that something may be. Maybe it's because deep inside it's what we want, or maybe we are afraid to lose what we don't really have. The thought and feeling of having nothing can steer us back to what we should have let go. I preach to be fearless and patient because what's out there will find its way as long as we work hard to better ourselves and grow as individuals.

Let's look at the emotions you feel the most—fear, anger, sadness, and joy. In my opinion, fear is all in the mind—with the exception of random circumstances when you are confronted with danger—so if you understand that, you can then learn to control that emotion and not be afraid of anything! If we can face our fears, we can beat them and minimize them just like in the movie *"IT."* Fearing nothing doesn't mean becoming foolhardy, however. It means knowing that you can face anything that comes your way. You will not be able to run away from your fears because you cannot run away from your thoughts.

Let's just say fear is gone, just for the sake of this discussion. Now that only leaves three emotions. We know anger can be controlled. Ask yourself, "What do I gain by becoming angry? Is this joke really that bad? Is my ego really tarnished?" Do not accept disrespect but treat rudeness and ill will with kindness. Do not respond with the same negative energy. It serves no purpose. Be the bigger person, only your ego is affected, not you because in a few days you probably will laugh over what you were angry about in the first place. Learn to control your anger. If the hulk can control his anger, then you should be okay, do your best.

Now let's say anger is gone as well, that leaves sadness and joy. Sadness is tougher than fear and anger because there are times when we can't control sadness, like when tears keep coming down. Pain hurts, but staying positive even through the darkest hours will help a lot. Being negative will do nothing for you. It is ok to be sad. After a time, when we are the saddest, is when we can become the most joyous. Do not erase sadness like anger and fear. Instead, combine it with joy by being positive and by understanding that *I may be in a bad situation or somebody close to me passed away*, but think of the good times and the best times yet to come. You are only as happy as your saddest child. If you didn't know what it was like to be sad, then how would you know what it is to be truly happy? Let joy consume your emotional life—no need to let the other three emotions hog up that much space. You cannot get rid of them, but you can control them a majority of the time, as they are a part of you.

You could ask what's the difference between joy and happiness. Some would say there is no difference. In my opinion, joy is a pregnant woman having a baby, while happiness is the process of being and getting pregnant.

> *"The three factors that seem to have the greatest influence on increasing our happiness are our ability to reframe our situation more positively, our ability to experience gratitude, and our choice to be kind and generous"*
>
> - *Dalai Lama XIV*

Being emotionless will not help you through life. Live to enjoy the relationships you have with others who cherish and care about you. You will meet some who will hurt you, but don't lose hope because eventually, you will meet those who truly love you. You can try to mask your emotions all you want, but as long as you live, your emotions will live as well.

The more control you have of your emotions, the less meaningless fights you take part in. Staying positive makes sense in that it creates positive outcomes. We all face challenges, and how we address them gives a chance to solve them and grow into the next level of our being.

Express Your Emotions

It's ok to be sad, mad, frustrated, and/or down. Yell at the top of your lungs, cry like a waterfall, and sulk in the place you love best. Let it out; don't keep your emotions bottled in. They will not fade away but will only haunt you until you cope with them.

Often, we think that our trials and tribulations are a nightmare, yet we know its reality, we just don't want to believe it. It's ok to be sympathetic but find a goal through tough times, find a purpose, don't let the suffering you endure go to waste. Channel that energy into something positive. Life is a long journey; focusing on the mini-milestones day by day helps smooths the path. Many times, we want to be on top of the staircase and fail to see the steps and only the top. Remember to take pride in each step you take on your journey to the top. We become so engulfed in the top that we fail to see how far we have come and what good we have done. Think of suffering and maliciousness as your chrysalis phase, and when you overcome, it's as if you are reborn, which is why the butterfly is a great beacon. Our life is full of caterpillar stages, and it's up to us to become a butterfly each and every time. When we stay in our chrysalis, it's easier to get knocked down even further, so might as well fight it while you are still able to and always persevere. You will be stronger physically and mentally, and you will notice how beautiful and how much more appreciative of life you will be.

If you need help, get it. Many don't because of the stigma associated with therapy. Therapy is not just for crazy people, it's for everyone. Expressing our problems is good for the soul. It helps us cope with them because if we can converse about them, then we are one step closer to accepting them.

Why is it that when we get really stressed out that there's a chance for us to get sick? I think it's having too many things bottled in, and it needs to be released. Look at yourself, for example, as a bottle and stress would be a liquid. The size of the bottle determines how much stress you can hold, but when stress starts to overflow, the bottle has reached its limit. So, let it go. Whether the stress is caused by a loss, love, failed an exam, or didn't make the team, there will be better days. It sucks, but don't let it take you over. Pain may win a battle or two, but don't let it win the war.

Fear Leads to Anger

"Fear is not evil. It tells you what your weakness is. And once you know your weakness, you can become stronger, as well as kinder."

- *Gildarts Clive (Hiro Mashima)*

You say you want to go to heaven, but you're afraid to die. Fear nothing, not even death, as it is a part of life. When you are not afraid of death, then you are free to live. Culture show guest Diana Anthill said there is, after all, absolutely nothing that doesn't follow the pattern of starting, developing, wearing out, and ending. Not a person, not an animal, not a plant, not a thing that ever was, is or will be, has failed to follow that pattern. Even things seeming to us eternal, such as mountains, gradually wear down – come to think of it, even planets die. It is simply how life works; death is a part of life.[34]

Don't be afraid of death; be afraid of an unlived life. You don't have to live forever; you just have to live. Leave your legacy and enjoy every day—the good and bad.

Nelson Mandela said, *"I learned that courage was not the absence of fear, but the triumph over it.*

---
[34] https://www.radiotimes.com/news/2013-07-13/death-is-a-part-of-life-why-be-afraid/

The brave man is not he who does not feel afraid, but he who conquers that fear." I felt fear more times than I can remember, but I hid it, a mask of boldness. We all have fears; it's how we approach them that make a difference.

I'm going to break down fear in a few scenarios to help you understand how fear alters images in your brain to the worst possible scenario. People have a hard time letting go of their suffering. Out of a fear of the unknown, they prefer suffering that is familiar.

Fear caused by events of the past can cloud your judgement and turn you into somebody you are not. Fear can also prevent us from doing many things. Sadly, it's the things in life we don't do we will regret later. Take those risks and see if the grass is greener on the other side with your own eyes. If you live in fear, you aren't living—you are paralyzed. Build your strength to a point where this part of life doesn't faze you and think of it like another wall to climb. Facing your fears helps you grow stronger every day, but hiding behind the fear can cause you to lose out on great opportunities. You cannot run away from your fears but can strive to overcome them, but first, you must believe in yourself and your grind.

"I have learned over the years that when one's mind is made up, this diminishes fear; knowing what must be done does away with fear."

- *Rosa Parks*

For your next mission, I challenge you to face three fears before your next vacation or adventure and journal your experience.

Anger Leads to Hate

I remember I came across an interesting read about how a snake attacked a saw. It seems a snake entered a carpentry shop, and as it crawled to the corner, it went through a saw and hurt itself a little bit. At that time, the snake turned and bit the saw. When he bit the saw, he badly hurt his mouth. Then, not understanding what was happening to him and thinking that the saw was attacking him, he decided to roll around the saw as if wanting to suffocate it with his whole body and shook the saw with all his strength. You can see what the outcome was here... It was unfortunate the snake ended up being killed by the saw. Sometimes we react in anger, thinking about hurting those who hurt us, but we are hurting ourselves.

"When we confront a challenge we often act to the situation with fear and anger."[35] Desmond Tutu and Dalai Lama wrote: *Especially today; there is not much focus on inner values in education. Then, instead of inner values, we become self-centered, always thinking: A self-centered attitude brings a sense of insecurity and fear. Distrust. Too much fear brings frustration. Too much frustration brings anger. So that's the psychology, the system of mind, of emotion, which creates a chain reaction.*[36]

When others try and make you angry, try to put things into perspective; if it doesn't really matter or directly affect you, why does it bother you? Every time you get upset at something, ask yourself if you were to die tomorrow, was it worth wasting your time being angry? Anger doesn't solve anything. It builds nothing, but it can destroy everything.

Anger isn't always a bad thing as it can fuel your work ethic or passion. It also protects your impeccable word if it has been disrespected. Happy go lucky is not always the answer. Expressing anger in a healthy way is a necessity. It's all about

---

[35] Qualities of the Heart and Mind - Kevin Pokorny Consulting. https://pokornyconsulting.com/qualities-heart-mind/
[36] His Holiness the Dalai Lama; Archbishop Desmond Tutu; Douglas Abrams; The Book of Joy; Lasting Happiness in a Changing World; Avery, New York, New York; Sept. 2016

controlling it and knowing when and when not to use it

> "Anger is the inner child taking its power back. Anger is protection, self-defense, the awakening that you are a divine being of worth and value. Do not be ashamed about your anger. Honor it. Love it. Validate it. Use it constructively as fuel to dream bigger loves yourself harder and accomplish your goals. Anger is the voice that says, you deserve the very best"
>
> - *Shahida Arabi*

Righteous anger is anger that is chosen in support of others and a tool of justice and compassion as opposed to a reactive emotion that is about the self.[37]

Have you ever been in an argument with someone you care about? How did it make you feel? Upset, powerful? Did you win or lose? If you were angry, I bet you lost. Transactional Analysis teaches us that there are three different forms of communication. These are:

> Parent – controlling
  o Authoritative style assuming control or superior knowledge
> Adult - Rational

---

[37] His Holiness the Dalai Lama; Archbishop Desmond Tutu; Douglas Abrams; The Book of Joy; Lasting Happiness in a Changing World; Avery, New York, New York; Sept. 2016

- Respectful style that allows different perspectives without judgment. This style is rational and unemotional; useful for discussions and co-operative planning.
> Child – Rebellious or Obedient
- Spontaneous and can be irresponsible.

Within these are multiple ways of communicating:

> Parent to Parent
> Parent to Child
> Adult to Adult
> Child to Child

You can see now that if you lose rationality, you won't win. Before getting into an argument, consider the following:

1. Is it important to me?
   a. Weigh out the consequences and benefits of the argument win or lose.
2. Have a discussion, not an argument
   a. Arguments are controlled by emotions; discussions are controlled by facts and opinions.
3. Ask questions

      a. Understanding someone else's point of view may change your own perceptions.
4. Understand that no one is you
      a. We all have unique experiences that influence our perspectives.
5. Mend old wounds
      a. Have closure to your arguments. An argument that is unresolved will fester.

Dale Carnegie once wrote, "The only way to get the best of an argument is to avoid it."[38] The hard part is that it takes more character to not say anything than to engage in the argument.

Sadness the Alienated Variable

"Nobody notices your sadness, nobody notices your tears, nobody notices your pain, but everyone notices your mistakes"

- *Harry Styles*

You don't cry in front of others to not look weak, yet with this façade on, how can others see how broken you may be or feel. Our sadness is critical to our empathy and compassion. It is normal to feel sad. We all go through a breaking point when things keep

---

[38] Carnegie, Dale; How to Win People and Influence People; Pocketbook Press, NY, NY; ©1998

happening that are not in our favor. I am here to tell you to keep on going as what you are going through is training you to be who you were meant to be.

Three feelings associated with sadness are despair, loneliness, and grief. We touched a bit on these earlier when we talked about depression and loneliness, but to me, these three feelings are some of the most imperative to grasp.

Despair means we've lost all hope and have basically given up. Loneliness is exactly what it says—alone. We can also be alone in a crowded room, not understanding that we are not the only ones going through whatever the current loneliness is caused by. Grief is most difficult as there is a tangible loss, whether it is a beloved pet, husband, wife, grandmother, grandfather, parent, and the list goes on.

> *"A strong person is not the one who doesn't cry. A strong person is the one who cries and sheds tears for a moment, then gets up and fights again."*

Unfortunately, life guarantees these experiences. No one is immune or singled out. Remember to laugh and smile at least once every day, even though the sad times. It is ok to feel fear, anger, and sadness but do not hold on to it, make way for new feelings.

You can cry, forgive, learn, and move on. Let your tears water the seeds of your future happiness. In order to move on we have to allow ourselves to go through the full gamut of emotions.

Chapter 8

Bearing the Risk

"Love is the reason why there is pain. When we lose someone precious to us, hate is born. Vengeance is the product of that hate and so death follows. But in death there is only more death. This will give rise to more pains. In this cursed world we live in, it is a cycle of hatred that will not cease."

- Pain (Masashi Kishimoto)

Heart of Love

What is it that you feel in your heart when you close your eyes? What is it that is precious and passionate to you? What is it that you think about when you wake up and go to sleep? What you truly love is always on your mind.

When you love something, it can bring you a lot of joy. When people love playing a sport, the feeling they get is like no other. Love is similar in that there is no other feeling. Love is very powerful. It can change people, make, and or break a person. It sucks that something so beautiful can breed much hatred. Those with the biggest hearts seem to get hurt the most. Some say love is a choice, while others will say it is not. There are some who love a person that they wish they didn't. Yet there are others who just want someone to love. When love acts negatively, do not let it overcome who you are. When we lose the love of our life or someone we loved that was close to us, it may be hard to cope with, but understand time heals all wounds with hard work and acknowledgment. It may be tough now, but you will get through this.

Love is also considered the most powerful feeling because sometimes we can't control it. We stay in toxic relationships because of love. Even when we aren't fully happy, love can keep us there. The only way to cope with love is to face it head-on and be truthful with yourself. Love can be the path to hatred, but it is also a path to a joyous life. The decisions you make and experience alter this path. If love hurt you, then the fear of being hurt will hinder you from fully loving another person. This can alter the path to your future. My roommate asked if I could go back in time to reverse heartbreak, would I? I said no because I wouldn't be who I am without it. The suffering I endured gave me answers to questions when I hit rock bottom. It was those answers that made me realize so much about life and myself as an individual. So why would I reverse growth?

Isn't it funny how one day you can say how much you love a person then a year goes by and you may not even talk to that person anymore? You know, I believe that everybody has a soul mate. If you keep going through the same type of relationships and expecting different results, then you're probably going to be very disappointed. There's a reason why the previous relationships didn't work. We are so fast to point the finger and use others as a scapegoat even though the real problem dwells within us. We don't want to face reality because we're scared! Some people run away from the truth but if you aren't truthful with yourself, then you will never be able to find true love. You can try and hide your emotions all you want but that's all you can do is hide them, they are still there and will eventually come out to play. Build yourself up, become the best version and love will find its way to you. If the person you are with doesn't feel lucky to have you and you them, then they aren't the one. All relationships are learning experiences. When they end, it's hard but it's the truth.

"When you lose sight of your path, look for the destination in your heart"

- *Allen Walker (Katsura Hoshino)*

Love is the third of Maslow's hierarchy of human need. We all need it; we all want it. But, love is like a garden; you have to tend to it for it to grow. How long has it been since you've told someone you loved them? How many people, whether family or friend, have you not seen in a while and haven't bothered to tell them, I love you? I encourage you now to reach out to two people that you haven't in a while and tell them that you love them.

Hate Leads to Suffering

Hatred is defined as an emotion and can evoke fear, animosity, or anger that can be directed at groups, entities, individuals, ideas, objects, behaviors, and/or concepts.[39] Robert Sternberg saw three components in hatred:

> 1. a negation of intimacy, by creating distance when closeness had become threatening;

---

[39] Reber, A.S., & Reber, E.; (2002). The Penguin Dictionary of Psychology; Penguin; New York, New York.

2. an infusion of passion, such as fear or anger;
3. a decision to devalue a previously valued object.[40]

Freud further defined hate as an ego state that wishes to destroy the source of its unhappiness, stressing that it was linked to the question of self-preservation.[41]

Hate is very often the lead story in the daily news. We demonize those who don't share our views, and that is a driving force behind a lot of daily human suffering that we put upon ourselves. It doesn't matter who we're talking about, if they've done something we disagree with whether they are a minority group or rhetoric espoused by politicians trying to get votes, it's part of the day.

Ever wonder where it all comes from? The origins of hate are not far from the origins of love. Love is said to generate from the heart, but new studies using functional magnetic resonance imaging, shows that strong emotions like love and hate start in the

---

[40] Ito ed., Encyclopedia of Emotion (2010) p 302
[41] S. Freud, "The instincts and the vicissitudes' (1915) in On Metapsychology (PFL 11) p. 135-5.

brain.[42] Going further, he assigns positive attributes to our in-group and negative to our outgroup. Psychologist call this the *ultimate attribution error*.[43] Hence, the origins of hate.

Hate can be equated to venom that poisons your heart and soul, damages relationships, and ultimately, us. Anyone who's truly hated can tell you how all-consuming this toxic emotion is. The word itself is very powerful. Think about how it felt when someone said, "I hate you." Think about what your intention was the first time you said, "I hate you," to your parent(s).

Ask yourself this question:

1. Does hate have a place in my life?
2. Do I hate anyone?
3. Do I hate myself?

If you've answered yes to any of those questions, please, address it before it destroys. Understand that "destroy" is not a matter of "if," it's a matter of "when."

---

[42] Harmon, Katherine; The Origins of Hate; Scientific American; August 2009.
[43] https://www.alleydog.com/glossary/definition. r

When you keep hatred inside for too long, resisting forgiving or letting go of the past, then you will turn into a monster. It will consume all your other emotions and can turn you into a manipulative by myself type of person. You will close your heart in fear of getting hurt. You can become fake and not true to even yourself. You may see success, but when you get there you will be all alone. Hatred can fuel your goals, yet for all the wrong reasons you may achieve them.

Hatred can sometimes give birth strength and power, but do not let that change you into something you are not. Do not let hate and revenge drive you to a dark place. It is never too late to turn around. Channel that hate into motivation. I'll use the example of being cut from a team again. Rather than focus your energy on hating the coach, focus on being a better player so that your coach will think twice about having cut you in the first place. In doing this, when the grind is complete, that hatred is no longer needed, and you'll see by re-channeling, you became a better and stronger person.

There are basically two types of hate – internal (implosion) where the hate is directed inward, and external (explosion) where the hate is directed outward. Hate turned outward is dangerous. It can lead to violent crimes and other destructive behavior. An example of this would be the shooting at the L.A. Fitness gym in Philadelphia. The gunman's hatred of women created by his perceived rejection by them fueled his anger and desperation, taking a great toll on life.

Vengeance is not the answer either. It only leads toward more hatred within yourself and those you seek revenge against. Think about it, if someone has a different opinion, is it worth hating them? Case and point, there was so much hate toward the leaders of the Civil Rights Movement, vengeance was sought to silence the voices. Some of the most well-known African American vocal leaders in the previous generations were killed, and never saw old age? Martin Luther King was shot over his own opinion. Tupac rapped his opinion and he was shot multiple times.

Do not waste part of your life hating something which is not relevant to your overall goal. Hating other people accomplishes nothing. Think about it, what has been angry or hating someone done for you? Does it really make you feel better?

It is ok to dislike a person or not associate yourself with them but why hate them? They've already had a negative effect on you, why perpetuate it? Let it go. Forgive but do not forget. Show kindness when others show hatred. Surround yourself with people who have good vibes.

Birth of Hate

> *"No one is born hating another person because of the color of his skin, or his background, or his religion. People must learn to hate, and if they can learn to hate, they can be taught to love, for love comes more naturally to the human heart than its opposite."*
>
> *- Nelson Mandela*

While anger can be resolved and fades with time, hate at its extreme is an enduring, inflexible state, an all-consuming set of raw emotions.[44] For those whose hate is not yet all-consuming, here are some steps to help resolve those feelings from a societal standpoint.

> \> Understand that hate is extremely destructive, whichever way you cut it, by recognizing the serious threat that hate creates for our personal, communal, and national well-being.

---

[44] Rapgay, Lobsang, Ph.D; The Psychology of Hate; Psychology Today; March 2018; https://www.psychologytoday.com/intl/blog/anxiety-fear-and-hate/201803/the-psychology-hate

> Learn to spot stereotyping, scapegoating, and de-humanizing behavior in ourselves, in others, and in certain leaders, so that we can start challenging such prejudiced verbal and non-verbal behavior.
> When you find yourself blaming an entire group, challenge that perception by conducting a comprehensive analysis of your behavior.
> Challenge the underlying beliefs and assumptions that maintain this toxic behavior.
> Make a list of evidence for and against your own beliefs and assumptions. Based on the conclusion of the analysis, replace your maladaptive beliefs and assumptions with ones that are more realistic and adaptive.
> Take concrete steps to re-educate yourself by reading and watching objective-based information. Evaluate the issues from the viewpoint of both sides – don't just listen to what you would like to hear.[45]

From a spiritual perspective, love is the only thing that can drive out hatred. When a person is mad or rude or disrespectful, show him kindness and see what happens. You will see the difference in

---
[45] see 17

communicating. Nobody is born to hate; you can only learn that. Nobody has ever looked at a baby and said what an evil baby. We are taught to love and hate. People with hatred were not always like that. Try to understand them and be kind to them. You never know what you could say to somebody that may not only change their day, week or month, but maybe even their life.

> *Hate cannot drive out hate; only love can do that.*
>
> *Dr. Martin Luther King, Jr.*

Heart of Evil

No one is born evil. Birth is one of the most joyous times in life.

Nobody is born evil, but some are raised in evil environments. It's often the circumstances and the person's nature that lead to his eventual behavior. Have you ever heard anybody say, damn that baby looks evil? No, because babies are full of laughter and crying. New life is full of happy and sad. Sadness will go away just like when a baby cries, he eventually stops, but the happiness remains. We are meant to be happy and fulfill our potential, but we must first overcome ourselves. Evil will try and trick you throughout life. It will try and feed negative, selfish, greedy thoughts into your head. Be selfless and caring, no matter the situation. Being negative will solve nothing. Being positive may not solve anything either, but it will keep hope alive for a better day. There will be people who do dirty things to you but forgive them, do not hate them.

> *"All it takes is one bad day to reduce the sanest man alive to lunacy. That's how far the world is from where I am. Just one bad day. You had a bad day once, am I right? I know I am. I can tell. You had a bad day and everything changed. "*
>
> *- Joker*

An interesting point about inherent evil or "response to circumstance" evil would be the DC character The Joker in the Batman Series. One of the backstories depicts him as an engineer who quit his job to become a stand-up comedian only to fail. He becomes desperate to support his pregnant wife and agrees to help plan a robbery of the plant he used to work at. During the planning, police contact him to tell him his wife and unborn child have died in an accident at home. He tried to back out of helping in the crime but had no option out. In the course of the robbery, they are caught, and the two criminals are killed. The engineer jumps into a vat of some type of chemical in his escape. When he later looks at himself in the mirror, his appearance is now grotesque. The culmination of these events caused a major personality shift and thus was born the Joker.[46] This scenario validates the argument that people are not born evil.

Now not everyone would seep to such destruction and chaos, but a step toward the wrong path can lead us down a wary journey. As this may be fictional, you can still intertwine his story with real-life events in the world as the catalyst in Joker's story could be something different in your story. My point is to depict how one bad day, one bad decision can lead to a life of misfortune.

So, what was his mistake? Why was destiny so cruel to him? Why was the world so cruel to him? Could he have prevented his wife or unborn child from dying? I see victims of circumstance and consequences of bad decisions happen to so many people around me. Their souls are crushed, emotions are hurt, and their feelings are smashed. They can't do anything about it because they are incapable at the time. What would you do if given the same set of circumstances? The Joker was not born, he was made.

---

[46] https://jester.fandom.com/wiki/The_Joker

Could that outcome have been averted? Perhaps before quitting his job, he should have pursued his dream on the side until it was big enough to support him. The lesson to learn here is not to be in such a rush. Our decisions play a huge part in who we are and how the outcome of our future. It is critical to think about the decisions we make and what the possible outcomes may be.

I believe in goodness. I never appreciated Joker before, and then something similar happened. When you have only one thing in the world, and you just want to live your life with that one thing, all your emotions and happiness are attached to that very thing. When you are denied that thing, and you feel you've never asked for anything in your whole life, you have choices to make—become a victim or rise above it.

Chapter 9

Leverage your Anguish

"The dark side will devour those who lack the power to control it. It's a fierce storm of emotions that annihilates anything in its path. It lays waste to the weak and unworthy. But those who are strong can ride the storm winds to unfathomable heights. They can unlock their true potential; they can sever the chains that bind them; they can dominate the world around them."

- *Darth Bane (George Lucas)*

Origin of Suffering

Suffering means submit to or forced to endure. Buddha assigned 4 truths to the origins of suffering:

1. The truth of suffering
2. The truth of the origin of suffering
3. The truth of the cessation of suffering
4. The truth of the path to the cessation of suffering[47]

These are known as the Four Noble Truths. It's interesting to note that something that was studied 2500 years ago is still true now.

---

[47] The Four Noble Truths; BBC © 2014; https:\\www.bbc.co.uk

There are many kinds of suffering, but there are some basics – those that most of us will have to deal with at some point. Those are old age, sickness, and death. But suffering goes further than that. Life isn't perfect and doesn't always live up to our expectations. As humans, we have desires and cravings, and even if we can satisfy them, often, it's only short-lived ultimately leaving us unfilled and unsatisfied. That is the truth of suffering.

Buddha also taught that suffering comes from desire and that desire has 3 roots:

1. Greed and desire
2. Ignorance or delusion
3. Hatred and destructive urges

It is clear from what philosophers and religious leaders have taught us; we create most of our suffering. It would be a logical assumption then that we also have the ability to create more joy. It depends on the attitudes, perspectives, and the reactions we have to situations and relationships with other people. If we are aware of these, then there is some degree of suffering we can control.

Is Suffering Necessary?

If you had not suffered as you have, there would be no depth to you as a human being, no humility, no compassion. You would not be reading this now.

- *Eckhart Tolle*

Is suffering necessary? Yes and no. As Tolle eloquently stated, suffering is part of what makes us who we are. We need suffering to appreciate joy, to grow and learn. Suffering can embitter or ennoble.[48] The choice is ours. The difference between being embittered or ennobled is if we can find meaning in our suffering. A great example of finding meaning in suffering was Nelson Mandela. Mr. Mandela endured 27 years in prison but still found ways to grow. He earned a law degree through a University of London correspondence program. Mr. Mandela continued to be outspoken against apartheid and never forfeit his convictions in exchange for freedom.

If it wasn't for our suffering, we wouldn't be who we are today. We can never let one tragedy stop us from moving forward in life. A lot of our suffering stems from things we love being taking away in our

---

[48] His Holiness the Dalai Lama; Archbishop Desmond Tutu; Douglas Abrams; The Book of Joy; Lasting Happiness in a Changing World; Avery, New York, New York; Sept. 2016

environment, or things that we can't accept. Suffering also stems from how we handle the origin of the pain. Suffering grows from our reaction to the original pain. More simply put, suffering is due to clinging or resisting, unwillingness to move, to flow with life, and letting go. These things have already taken so much from us, why then should we let them take our peace of mind?

Suffering and pain aren't always bad as the payoff can be astronomical. Think about when we go to the gym or workout. We put ourselves through hell and almost push ourselves to the point where we can't walk. Why do we endure this? The answer is simple—for the end result. We feel stronger and look our best. We've gained a certain degree of satisfaction knowing we've reached past our limit.

When we suffer, it is best not to be distracted by others who would lead us off the path. Perhaps they'll tell us we are weak, or silly, or there's no point. Only we can decide those things for ourselves. Keeping our eye on the payout or end results and stay the course is the best way to focus our thoughts and not those of others.

We must be able to think things through—determine what's at the root of our suffering when it isn't obvious (like going to the gym). What's also important to remember is not to overthink things. Often times our suffering can be a result of our imagination rather than from reality. Overthinking consumes our mind then controls our life.

Ah, so much easier said than done, but it's possible. Don't overstress about things, don't obsess, and don't beat yourself up. Instead, enjoy the moments of every day. Don't cloud your head with negative thoughts and unnecessary worry. Focus on the moments, no matter how simple. It could be something as small as savoring your favorite cup of coffee or tea, noticing the smell of fresh-cut grass, adoring the sunset, or chatting with your best friend.

Mother Nature is her own entity, and we cannot stop the suffering of natural disasters as they are out of our control, but so much of the rest of our suffering, we can stop. Natural Disasters is the villain that the world needs. To see so much destruction allows us to cherish what it is we have. We have become so innovated that we can predict when it will occur as we can save millions at the cost of being reminded how grateful each day is.

Since we create most of our suffering in our minds and our perspectives in and of life, learning to choose your battles will go a long way to reducing stress and suffering.

There are several ways to help reduce stress and suffering. The 16 most common ways are:

- Exercise - It may sound counterintuitive, but regular exercise can help lower stress and anxiety by releasing endorphins and improving your sleep and self-image.
- Consider Supplements - Certain supplements can reduce stress and anxiety, including ashwagandha, omega-3 fatty acids, green tea and lemon balm.
- Light a Candle - Aromatherapy can help lower anxiety and stress. Light a candle or use essential oils to benefit from calming scents.
- Reduce Caffeine Intake - High quantities of caffeine can increase stress and anxiety. However, people's sensitivity to caffeine can vary greatly.
- Write it down - Keeping a journal can help relieve stress and anxiety, especially if you focus on the positive.
- Chew Gum - According to several studies, chewing gum may help you relax. It may also promote wellbeing and reduce stress.

- Spend Time with Family and Friends - Having strong social ties may help you get through stressful times and lower your risk of anxiety.
- Laugh - Find the humor in everyday life, spend time with funny friends or watch a comedy show to help relieve stress.
- Learn to Say No - Try not to take on more than you can handle. Saying no is one way to control your stressors.
- Learn to Avoid Procrastination - Prioritize what needs to get done and make time for it. Staying on top of your to-do list can help ward off procrastination-related stress.
- Take a Yoga Class - Yoga is widely used for stress reduction. It may help lower stress hormone levels and blood pressure.
- Practice Mindfulness - Mindfulness practices can help lower symptoms of anxiety and depression.
- Cuddle - Positive touch from cuddling, hugging, kissing and sex may help lower stress by releasing oxytocin and lowering blood pressure.
- Listen to Soothing Music - Listening to music you like can be a good way to relieve stress.

- Deep Breathing- Deep breathing activates the relaxation response. Multiple methods can help you learn how to breathe deeply.
- Spend Time with your Pet - Spending time with your pet is a relaxing, enjoyable way to reduce stress.[49]

Although stress and anxiety may come up in your workplace and personal life, there are many simple ways to reduce the pressure. These tips involve getting your mind away from the source of stress. Exercise, mindfulness, music and physical intimacy can all work to relieve anxiety which will help balance your work and personal life

Coping with Pain

"A lesson without pain is meaningless, for you cannot gain something without sacrificing something else in return. But once you have recovered it and made it your own. You will gain an irreplaceable full metal heart."

- *Edward Ulric (Hiromu Arakawa)*

Life is full of scrapes, bumps, and bruises. It goes along with the ride, and there's no way to avoid it. It's like learning to ride a bike; it's not *if* we fall but rather *when* we fall. When it happens, we cry, brush

---

[49] https://www.healthline.com/nutrition/16-ways-relieve-stress-anxiety

ourselves off, get a hug from mom or dad, and everything is right again. Coping with the scrapes in life is different, but when we fall, we still have to get back up again.

The difference between physical scrapes and bruises and emotional injuries is that the physical ones are eventually healed by the wonderful mechanisms of our human body. Unfortunately, the emotional ones are not so easy. To understand how to cope with emotional injuries, it is helpful to understand how we are hurt in the first place. In Guy Winch's book *"Emotional First Aid,"* he talks about the seven sources of emotional injuries.

1. Cuts and scrapes caused by rejection
2. The relationship muscle weakness of loneliness
3. Broken bones of loss and trauma
4. The poisonous effect of guilt
5. Emotional scars of rumination
6. The psychological pneumonia of failure
7. Low self-esteem's danger to your emotional immunity[50]

---

[50] Winch, Guy Ph.D.; Emotional First Aid: Healing Rejection, Guilt, Failure; Plume; reprint edition; July 2014

> *"We think sometimes that poverty is only being hungry, naked and homeless. The poverty of being unwanted, unloved and uncared for is the greatest poverty."*
>
> *- Mother Theresa*

Coping with these emotional injuries is more difficult in part because of the drain it creates when we are trying to find a solution. In fact, coping mechanisms that are usually helpful can deteriorate into rumination. Most people have, at some point, experienced obsessing over something stressful. When these thoughts turn more negative and brooding, that's known as rumination.

Rumination usually starts off fairly benignly but escalates. This can drag you into a self-perpetuating loop of stress and frustration. And of course, that takes its toll as well. So, how then do we cope? Fortunately, while we can't always fix the problem overnight, we can lessen the emotional stress and the toll it takes on us. Elizabeth Scott, MS offers these 4 coping exercises:

- **Practice Mindfulness** - When we feel emotional stress, it's also often experienced as physical pain. It's common to try to escape these feelings, but it can be helpful to go deeper into the experience and use mindfulness to really notice where these emotional responses are felt physically.

- **Distract Yourself** - It's also been discovered that distracting oneself from emotional pain with emotionally healthy alternatives—such as a feel-good movie, fun activities with friends, or a satisfying mental challenge—can lessen emotional pain and help us feel better.

- **Block off Some Time** - If you find that emotional stress and rumination creep into your awareness quite a bit, and distraction doesn't work, try scheduling some time—an hour a day, perhaps—where you allow yourself to think about your situation fully and mull over solutions, concoct hypothetical possibilities, replay upsetting exchanges, or whatever you feel the emotional urge to do. Journaling is a great technique to try here, especially if it's done as both an exploration of your inner emotional world and an exploration of potential solutions. Talk to your friends about the problem, if you'd like. Fully immerse yourself. And *then* try some healthy distractions. This technique works well for two reasons:

- o If you really have the urge to obsess, this allows you to satisfy that craving in a limited context.
- o You may find yourself more relaxed the rest of the day because you know that there will be a time to focus on your emotional situation; that time is just later.
- **Practice Meditation** - Meditation is very helpful for dealing with a variety of stressors, and emotional stress is definitely in the category of stressors that meditation helps with. It allows you to take a break from rumination by actively redirecting your thoughts, and provides practice in choosing thoughts, which can help eliminate some emotional stress in the long term. Try a few meditation techniques today.

Whatever the cause of your stress, you can lessen and manage it. It will make you feel better and, as a result, help solve the problem.

What's the Point?

"You can't get back what you've lost, what's important now is what is it that you still have."

- *Jimbei (Eiichiro Oda)*

There are those who are constantly belittled, constantly struggling, constantly facing negativity, and constantly making mistakes. They begin to wonder if the rest of their life will be like this. While seeing others happy and living their best life especially on social media, can lead to those who feel dead inside yearn to make others feel the same way as them.

While there is no one reason for mass genocide or suicide, the pain of rejection, or the brunt of someone else's cruelty, is certainly one of them. If you feel like you have been hurt so much that suicide has crossed your mind, understand that it's a permanent solution for a temporary problem. Think about those who care about you and how they will walk this earth knowing somebody they love, took their life.

Why do we go to amusement parks when we know they will close? It's the thrill that gets us going, and life is no different. Ending things soon is like going to the amusement park and leaving because the lines are too long when that is just a part of being there.

I knew of a woman who worked 3 jobs at 52 years old and had two kids murdered but was still vibrant and happy. You could ask how and why when that doesn't sound like a happy life at all to the blind eye. She responded that life is full of blessings and tragedies, and we should never stand still but always continue to move forward. If we stay in one place because of a tragedy, then we cannot grow as a person, which is the same as dying as well. Death doesn't always have to lead to a negative life. There are blessings in disguise in a lot of things; it's up to u and how you perceive them.

You don't know about real loss that only occurs when you love something more than you love yourself."

- Robin Williams

There will always be pain in life. Only you have the power to release from its grip. You have to decide, and to stand up after you fall, then take necessary steps to heal. By staying down, you let pain defeat you. It is when you rise up against the pain you have released yourself. Once you have released it, move on and enjoy life."

Overcoming Revenge

All creations, humans, animals, and plants, have a "dark side." The rose, for example, is beautiful with bright-colored petals contrasted with deep green leaves. But it also has thorns—its dark side. When we refer to the dark side of humans, it usually referrers to our most aggressive, anti-social instincts.[51] That can be mean-spiritedness or even bloodthirsty belligerence buried somewhere within our psyche. While these things can include rape, murder, mutilation, and other unconscionable acts, for the purposes of this discussion, the darkness I am referring to is our unwillingness to share, to be kind, to be gentle; not the heinous acts of someone with psychopathological issues.

> *"Darkness... When everything that you know and love... is taken from you so harshly... all you can think about is anger, hatred, and even revenge... and no one can save you."*
>
> *- Orochimaru (Masashi Kishimoto)*

People can and will be cruel to us at different times and in different ways to us throughout our lives. It is unfortunate but true. How we react to these events can define us. Understanding how emotions and

---
[51] https://www.psychologytoday.com/us/blog/evolution-the-self/201412/just-how-dark-is-your-dark-side

thoughts influence our behavior is important. This is especially true for those who are ruled by their emotions. Knowledge about emotions and the thoughts that strengthen or soften them can help develop ways to manage actions better.

When we are "wronged," a gut response is to seek revenge. Webster's online dictionary defines revenge as to avenge (as oneself) *usually by retaliating in kind or degree or to inflict injury in return for something,* such as to revenge an insult.[52]

> *"Pirates are evil? The marines are righteous? These terms have always changed throughout history. Kids who have never seen peace and kids who have never seen war have entirely different values. Those who stand up at the top determine what's wrong and what's right. This very place is neutral ground! Justice will prevail you say? But of course, it will. Whoever wins this war becomes justice."*
>
> *- Donquixote Doflamingo (Eiichiro Oda)*

We seek revenge in the name of justice as those who wronged us deserve to be taken care of. But if revenge is called justice, then that justice breeds yet more revenge, thus, the chain of hatred has formed intertwining each other life by life. In order to break

---

[52] https://www.merriam-webster.com/dictionary/revenge

this chain, it takes a tremendously forgiving person to end this cycle of hatred.

Revenge has been part of the human response since the dawn of time. Even Shakespeare said, "If you prick us do, we not bleed? If you tickle us do, we not laugh? If you poison us do, we not die? And if you wrong us shall we not revenge?"[53] Apparently, Shakespeare thought revenge was perfectly normal. That may be true, but it is also self-destructive. Confucius said, "Before you embark on a journey of revenge, dig two graves." Gandhi shared this philosophy when he said, "An eye for an eye only ends up making the whole world blind."

We have all wanted "revenge" at some point in our lives. Who has not said, "I hope he gets his," or to quote Dirty Harry, "Go ahead, make my day"? It is a natural response. Theorist believes that revenge can be a protective and reinforcement mechanism. "If you don't turn down the music, I'm going to call the cops." Here, revenge is calling the cops. It gives the person saying it the power of a viable form of revenge. But is revenge the right way to respond?

---

[53] Shakespeare, William; The Merchant of Venice; Simon & Schuster; New York, New York; January 2009;

"Sweet is revenge," wrote Lord Byron (*Don Juan*, Canto I, Stanza 124). Indeed, this belief may be both venerable and wide-spread, but is it right? Kevin Carlsmith, a professor of sociology at Colgate University, did a study on revenge with several groups of college students. He devised a game where each group pooled an equal sum of money. One person in each group did not contribute. This

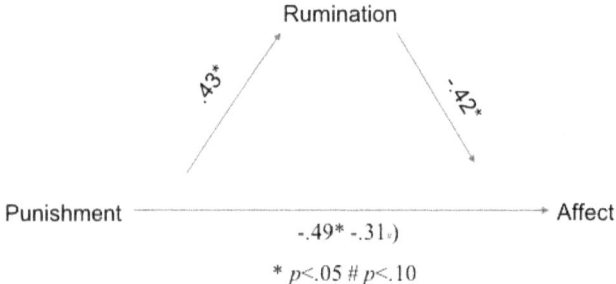

We anticipated, and found, a recursive relationship between affect and rumination such that each variable served as a partial mediator for the effect of punishment on the other. Thus, affect at Time 2 was related to both punishment (b ☒ ☒.49) and rumination (b ☒ ☒.40), and the direct effect of punishment on rumination was reduced when affect was included in the equation. The beta coefficient dropped from b ☒ .43 to .22, which was also marginally significant by the Sobel test (z ☒ 1.77, p ☒ .08).

changed the outcome of the share where those who'd invested made less than those who had not. What was interesting was that those who made more money felt bad or guilty, having cheated their group. The image above shows the results of the study.

In simple terms, this means that revenge makes us feel worse. So then, what do we do? I recommend treating people with kindness and working hard. Let success and karma be your weapon towards revenge.

When you show people kindness, the outcome can sometimes be confusion. Meaning, how can you be kind to me when I'm being evil to you? The confusion could shed new light and new answers as to the why. By responding through purity of heart, you have a better chance to help those around you, whether it is a friend, family member, acquaintance, or even an enemy.

It is unfortunate that negative things happen, but it is life, and we must learn to deal with it. Remember, there is no dark without light. As long as you keep hope alive and stay pure, the light will always penetrate through the darkness. Life is what you make of it. You can sulk and complain, but what will that accomplish? Absolutely nothing. From this day forward, whatever life throws at you, you know you can get through it. Start being kind today.

The Unbearable Task

"Suffer now enjoy later," is what my uncle told me. Sacrifice now and reap the benefits in the future like majoring in a tough subject as opposed to an easier one. While it may require more work and sacrifice now, you will see the results of your labor later in life. Don't get a college degree just to say you graduated college. Make the right choice for your future and not just the now. Plan your life. Graduating from college shouldn't be the highlight of your life but rather a steppingstone to something greater. Become somebody you never thought you could. See how far you can go, which will help to define the path to your purpose. You may not find it now or soon, but be on the lookout for some experiences that change your life and lead you to a purpose.

> *"Don't quit. Suffer now and live the rest of your life as a champion. Suffering is inevitable, it happens to all of us on its own time. Don't compare your pain to someone else's, especially as a scapegoat. Learn from it, grow from it, and experience it."*[54]
>
> - *Muhammad Ali*

---

[54] "Real Meaning behind Muhammad Ali's Words." The Triangle Tribune, vol. 20, no. 34, Charlotte Post Publishing Co., 2 Dec. 2018, p. 3A.

Realize that life goes on, bad things will happen, but you have to deal with them and live the next day. Challenge yourself and see if you can handle this stage of life as one day your kids may go through the same thing and ask for your advice.

Be so comfortable in yourself and who you are that you can laugh at yourself or even laugh with others who make fun of you. If someone has hurt you, don't long for an apology that's probably never going to come—move on. Be the bigger person because life becomes easier when you learn to accept an apology you never got.

There are those who have known true pain straight from birth. Being disowned by their parents, belittled by teachers and classmates, told they wouldn't amount to anything, beaten every day, molested, not given an equal chance, born a paraplegic, born with cancer or an infectious disease. I could keep going, but you get the point. Before you complain, take a step back and realize what you do have. Just because you may have had a bad past, doesn't mean that things won't change.

Please, I ask you not to lose faith in others because of what people have done to you. We need to learn, and unfortunately, sometimes it's through hurt. Look at Derrick Rose, who plays in the NBA. He kept getting hurt year after year, yet never gave up. There were days he wanted to quit, and people told him his career was over, but he didn't listen and kept believing in himself. That belief has transcended him to one of the greatest and respectable athletes today. He went from being traded over and over to adoring 50 points and being an all-star candidate last season.

No matter what you go through, keep working hard, and believing—the rest will take care of itself as long as you have faith.

Let all the pain and suffering out then form a plan to come back stronger, so that you never relive that pain again. One day you will laugh at the things that caused you suffering. Be flexible; always ready to change and keep moving forward. The light is at the end of the tunnel—it will not come to you.

> *"Character cannot be developed in ease and quiet. Only through experience of trial and suffering can the soul be strengthened, ambition inspired and success achieved."*
>
> *- Helen Keller*

We say we want to eradicate our demons as we believe once they are gone, we will be free. But it's quite the contrary. We never lose our demons, as we can only channel that darkness into a new strength and perspective. You cannot swim out of the current in a stream as it is too strong, but you can use that power as your own in order to swim faster. Later you may feel as that current was a blessing in disguise as our worst nightmares can intertwine with our best dreams.

Your scars may have been around more than some people in your life have. Understand that our suffering is relevant in the sense that it gave you a chance to overcome a new obstacle, which is prudent in becoming who we are supposed to become.

> *"Challenges are what make life interesting and overcoming them is what makes life meaningful."*
>
> *- Joshua J. Marine*

For the next mission, I challenge you to go 1 month acknowledging your suffering. Don't think about it, don't let others that remind you of your pain or make you feel sad. Rejoice in who you are. Be free of the shackles that brought you so much misery. Soar in life like how a hawk flies through the skies with no other bird.

Part III

Tranquility

X

Thrive

Chapter 10

Retrofitting the Mind

"Watch your thoughts; they become words. Watch your words; they become actions. Watch your actions; they become habits. Watch your habits; they become character. Watch your character; it becomes your destiny"

- Lao Tze

Outlook of the Mind

We often tend to think too small when we have a powerful weapon within us, which is our ideas and knowledge. Ideas and knowledge can't be taken away as they are bulletproof. You would be amazed at what you could do when you put your mind to it and have the right purpose to drive you. Our convictions may be untouchable, but our mind can act as a double-bladed sword. We have so many calamities of life, but nothing kills a person faster than their own mind.

How we approach things in life are thought processes. Those processes, or our outlook, affect the outcomes in our lives. It affects our health, our work, our relationships, and ultimately, our success. It is important to express our emotions without judgement or attachment. This will allow them to flow freely and not affect overall health. If you hold back your emotions, especially fear or negative emotions, it can affect physical and mental health.[55]

Positive emotions are important. A study done by scientist Barbara Fredrickson showed that positive emotions:

1. Broaden our perspective of the world
2. Build over time, creating lasting emotional resilience and flourishing.[56]

You can understand how this would affect our choices in finding our true path in life. So, how do we get there?

---

[55] https://www.takingcharge.csh.umn.edu/how-do-thoughts-and-emotions-affect-health
[56] Fredrickson, Barbara PhD.; Positivity; Three Rivers Press; New York, New York; © 2009

Immunity for the Mind

In the Urban dictionary, the Armored Mind is defined as: To protect one's ethics from being affected by mental pressure; to keep composure, determination and ethics from being mentally weakened.[57] This isn't to be confused with creating an emotional armor. You need to feel, love, cry, and laugh. What it means is to shut out the noise. Don't let the negative influences or skewed perceptions alter your path.

Let's look at perception. Most things are only different in the mind. When we are accustomed to being perceived a certain way, and we 'own' that image, it hurts when that feeling is gone or others don't look at us the same. Like wearing a specific style of clothing that generates a lot of compliments, it becomes hard to wear things that don't generate the same type of compliments. The person whose opinion is important is that person looking back at you in the mirror. You need to love yourself from within, and not let what's on the outside fuel your psyche.

57
https://www.urbandictionary.com/define.php?term=Mind%20Armor

"An entire sea of water can't sink a ship unless it gets inside the ship. Similarly, the negativity of the world can't put you down unless you allow it to get inside you."

- *Goi Nasu*

Life is not a walk in the park. Living with an armored mind can be very prudent when planning to tackle a new adventure. Life will throw numerous inconveniences, and if your mind is not strong enough, then just one inconvenience can deter you away from the overall goal. Stay strong, armor your mind, and live with immunity.

Training the Mind

You can train your mind to be able to endure anything. For example, you can train your mind to believe that you can do anything and are willing to do whatever it takes. When you believe, you can achieve.

A lot of times, we ask why when we don't have the things we want or aren't living the life we want. Stop asking why, instead, ask what's next? Train your mind to be prepared for anything. The more you overcome, the more used to it you will become. I have learned that when some problems occur, you will look in the past and may rejoice that it happened.

Look at the training Navy SEALS go through. They are tough-minded because they went through hell. If you can overcome your hell, then you can have the mentality of a Navy SEAL, but that mentality is not easy to gain. Sometimes, it requires going through excruciating hardships, but it's those hardships that catapult your mind to a higher level.

> *"Your life will not get straightened out until your mind does."* Train your mind to always be strong and positive.[58]
>
> -Joyce Meyers

Joyce Meyers, a well-known Christian minister in Missouri, once said, "Remember, you become what you think. Think discouraging thoughts, and you'll get discouraged." Thoughts are symbols that communicate what's going inside our minds, and as such, our thoughts influence how we feel about ourselves as well as how others may perceive us.

Our habitual thoughts and actions determine our destiny. If we think negatively and are filled with judgment about ourselves, then we are likely to

---

[58] Battlefield of The Mind Quotes by Joyce Meyer.
https://www.goodreads.com/work/quotes/246528-battlefield-of-the-mind-winning-the-battle-in-your-mind

follow through our thoughts with actions. If we think positively and take positive actions toward our goals, our destiny is far more likely to be happy. We may fall once or twice and get bruised, but if we make it a habit to get up, then we will be successful.

We spend a fair amount of time thinking about events of the past and worrying about the future, usually focused on things that have made us unhappy. Though this isn't uncommon, negative thoughts can prevent us from enjoying life, distract us from what's important, and in general, drain our energy.

If you find yourself in this vicious cycle, don't worry, it can be changed. There are seven ways to help manage these negative thoughts.

> **1. Recognize thought distortions.** Our minds have clever and persistent ways of convincing us of something that isn't really true. These inaccurate thoughts reinforce negative thinking. If you can recognize them, you can learn to challenge them. Here are four common thought distortions:

- *Black and white thinking.* Seeing everything as one way or another, without any in between.

- *Personalizing.* Assuming you are to blame for anything that goes wrong, like thinking someone did not smile at you because you did something to upset her. (It's more likely that person is having a hard day and her mood had nothing to do with you.)

- *Filter thinking.* Choosing to see only the negative side of a situation.

- *Catastrophizing.* Assuming the worst possible outcome is going to happen.

2. Challenge negative thoughts. Whenever you have a distorted thought, stop and evaluate whether it is accurate. Think about how you would respond if a friend spoke about herself that way. You would probably offer a good rebuttal to his or her negative view. Apply the same logic to your own thoughts. Ask yourself if you are assuming the worst will happen or blaming yourself for something that has not gone the way you wanted. And then think about other possible outcomes or reasons that something turned out differently than you hoped.

3. Take a break from negative thoughts. It is possible to learn how to separate from negative thoughts. One way to do this is to allow you a certain amount of time (maybe five minutes) with the thought. Then take a break from focusing on it and move on with your day.

4. Release judgment. We all judge ourselves and others, usually unconsciously. Constantly comparing ourselves to other people or comparing our lives to some ideal breed's dissatisfaction. When you are able to let go of judgment (not easy, but possible), you will likely feel more at ease. Some ways to take a break from judgmental thoughts include recognizing your own reaction, observing it, and then letting it go. Another helpful technique is to "positive judge." When you notice you are negatively judging a person, yourself, or a situation, look for a positive quality, too.

5. Practice gratitude. Research shows that feeling grateful has a big impact on your levels of positivity and happiness. Even when you are experiencing a challenging time in your life, you can usually find things (even small things) to be grateful for. Noticing the things that are going well and making you feel happy will keep you in touch with them. Keeping a gratitude journal and writing a few things in it every day is one easy and effective way to do this.

6. Focus on your strengths. It's human nature to dwell on the negative and overlook the positive. The more you can practice focusing on your strengths and not dwelling on mistakes you've made, the easier it will be to feel positive about yourself and the direction your life is taking. If you find yourself thinking harsh thoughts about your personality or actions, take a moment to stop and think about something you like about yourself.

7. Seek out professional support if you are unable to manage your thoughts or find they are interfering with your ability to meet your daily responsibilities or enjoy life. Counseling and therapy can help you weather life changes, reduce emotional suffering and experience self-growth.[59]

Healthy Body Healthy Mind

Studies have shown that exercise benefits not only the body but our mental health as well. Daily exercise brings a sense of well-being. We are more energetic, sleep better, feel more relaxed, and positive about ourselves and our lives. Exercise is one of the most powerful medicines. Try to exercise every day even if it's just for 45 minutes. It will give you a great type of feeling after. A feeling of bettering yourself. Do it enough times, and it will become a lifestyle.

Exercise—it is great for stress and just your overall health. Exercise can change your life, not only physically but mentally. You will notice how much happier you are by feeling the self-love. When you work out, you are looking better, feeling better, and all around have better energy around you. A day won't go by that you leave the gym unhappy. The gym will do wonders for things like anxiety, persistence, willpower, compassion toward others, appreciation for your body, and your overall outlook

---

[59] Patrician Hardeneck, PhD.: 7 Ways to Deal with Negative Thoughts; September 29, 2015;
https://www.psychologytoday.com/us/blog/women-s-mental-health-matters/201509/7-ways-deal-negative-thoughts

on life. When your mind, body, and spirit are one, great things begin to unfold.

Challenge yourself and grow every day. We don't know when our last day will be, so use every day wisely

As physical activity is to the body, are reading, learning, and writing great exercise for the mind. These can be healthy escapes from "reality" where we can assume perhaps the role of the protagonist in a great story, or release some tension writing about a situation. Learning can open whole new avenues for us. There's a world of exercise out there; be a part of it!

Talking Mind

Self-talk is your internal dialogue. It's influenced by your subconscious mind, and it reveals your thoughts, beliefs, questions, and ideas. Self-talk can be both negative and positive.

It's ok to talk to yourself. Contrary to popular belief, it doesn't mean you're crazy. We all have internal dialogues, and it's perfectly natural and healthy. Internal Self Talk includes positive and negative thoughts. A healthy ratio is considered to be two positive thoughts per one negative.[60] These dialogues that we have with ourselves influence our feelings and behaviors. It is important to keep a healthy dialogue. It's easy to beat ourselves up with negative thoughts. To help avoid that, we need to be able to identify the characteristics of the negative thoughts.

- Automatic (Just pop into your head without you choosing)
- Not based on accurate assessment
- Are unrealistic and unreasonable
- Seem totally believable
- Make us feel worse
- Unhelpful
- Persistent
- Partly based on a few, isolated facts
- Are not accurate
- Tend to be excessively pessimistic
- Can become a habit
- Serve no use

You're not crazy if you talk to yourself. In fact, your thoughts are "talking" to you all the time. And the way you talk to yourself is one of the most important things in your life. You can never get beyond what you think—especially what you think of yourself. What's important is not to get wrapped up in the negative. Dr. Magdalena Battles offers the following 15 tips to practice positive self-talk.

---

[60] Domar, Alice PhD.; Stress and Internal Self Talk; http://stresscourse.tripod.com/id101.html

1. Have a Higher Purpose Than Self?
   Having a strong faith in a higher power is helpful in having positive self-talk.
2. Cut Overly Negative People out of Your Life
   Everyone can have a down day and be negative or moody.
3. Be Grateful
   A great way to find the positive in your life and create positive self-talk, is to recognize the things in your life for which you can be grateful.
4. Don't Compare Yourself to Others
   When you are constantly comparing what you lack to what others have, you can easily get down on yourself.
5. Use Positive Words with Others
   If we are negative with our words with others, then we are likely to be negative about ourselves as well.
6. Believe in Your Success
   Believe in your ability to succeed. Believe in the abilities and skills that you have, so that you can propel yourself toward success.
7. Don't Fear Failure

Don't fear failure as it is often the road to success. Some of the greatest success stories in life are of people who failed multiple times before becoming successful.

8. Replace Negative Thoughts with Positive Ones
   Negative thoughts happen. It's hard to provide yourself with positive thoughts all the time.
9. Post Positive Affirmations

   A great way to provide positive self-talk to yourself is to write it down.

   Here are some examples that you can post on your bathroom mirror. (Use sticky notes):
   - I am adventurous and I am embracing all that life has to offer.
   - I feed my spirit daily.
   - I am in charge of how I feel today.
   - I am grateful for…
   - I will choose happiness and gratitude today.
   - I am special and unique, nobody else in the world is exactly like me.
   - I am proud of myself for…
   - I show love to myself and others daily in all that I do.
   - I find joy in all situations.
   - I am kind to others and to myself.
   - I am of value and have purpose in this world.
10. Don't Dwell in the Past

Don't be too hard on yourself. Everyone has a past. Everyone has bad things in their past.

11. Visualize Your Success

Your ability to visualize your success is tied to your ability to actually achieve success.

12. Limit Your Intake of the News and Media

The news and media can be predominantly negative.

13. Help Others

Helping others is a way to bless others, but it can also be an even bigger blessing to you.

14. Be Physically Active

There are a great many benefits to becoming active; such benefits include increased creativity, reduced anxiety, improved self-confidence, reduced stress, increase in happy brain chemicals and more.[61]

15. Dream and Set Goals

---

[61] Greatest: Benefits of Exercise; https://greatist.com/fitness/13-awesome-mental-health-benefits-exercise#1

> A great way to begin positive self-talk is to dream about the future.[62]

Self-talk and visualization are two keys to success. They are effective techniques for self-improvement, and for improving your life, because they imprint your intentions and desires on your subconscious mind, which in turn, helps you achieve them. So, go ahead, talk to yourself—you're not crazy!

State of Mind

Your mind is not just for thoughts or ideas. Mindsets exist around and below thought processes.

Don't let others dictate what you become. If you struggle in school, that doesn't mean college isn't for you. We all learn differently, but what I have come to understand is that sometimes, we need the right motivation. I graduated with an engineering degree and scored about 1000 on the SAT. I didn't like big exams because I would get bored halfway through. But I had the mindset to conquer anything I set my mind too, and sometimes that's all we need. Before you set your mind to do something, ask yourself if I'm doing this for me, money, or my parents. If you're doing it for the money and have no passion for it, you

---
[62] See 9

will be burning yourself out. If you're doing it for your parents, then is it to make you happy or them? Remember, this is your life, not theirs. If you're goals make your parents happy too, then that's great. But don't let guilt, not wanting to upset someone, or keeping the peace be your motivation. Again, at the end of the day, you're the one who's living your life.

> *"I see, now that the circumstance of life are irrelevant, what you do with the gift of life determines who you are."*
>
> - *Mewtwo (Takeshi Shudo)*

We can all be strong mentally, no matter who we are. All it takes is the right motivation to keep us going and the curiosity to see how far our work ethic can take us. I gave myself three options when it came to deciding a career; it was either a lawyer, doctor or engineer. I decided to pick three of the toughest majors in order to test myself, plus I wanted to live a lavish lifestyle. I wanted to do things my own way. If other people can do it, then why not me, was the question. By changing your thoughts and mindset, you can transform your life.

Our Intertwined Mind

The concept of mindset was discovered by Carol Dweck at Stanford. Dweck began her research on this topic by tackling a question: What happens if you give kids a difficult problem to solve? Some children viewed the problem as a challenge and learning experience. Other children felt that it was impossible to solve and that their intelligence was being held up for scrutiny and judgment.

The kids in the first group had growth mindsets. When faced with something difficult, they believed that they could learn and develop the skills they needed to solve it. The second group of kids had fixed mindsets. They believed that there was nothing they could do to tackle a problem that was out of the reach of their knowledge and abilities.[63]

Simply, mindset is whether you believe qualities like intelligence and talent are fixed traits or changeable. There are two types of mindset—fixed and growth. A person with a fixed mindset believes that these qualities are inherent, fixed, and cannot be changed. They also believe that talent alone creates success—without effort. They are dead wrong.

---

[63] https://www.verywellmind.com/what-is-a-mindset-2795025

Those with a growth mindset believe these abilities can be developed and strengthened through commitment and hard work. This perception creates a love of learning and strength essential for great achievements. All great people share these qualities.

> *"I want to free your mind but all I can do is show you the door, but it is you that must walk through it. Free your mind from doubt, disbelief and fear"*
> - The Matrix 1999 (Lana & Lilly Wachowski)

How Does a Mindset Form?

Dweck postulates that people are trained in the two mindsets at an early age by the way they are raised and their experiences at school.

> **Fixed Mindsets**

- Children who are taught that they should look smart instead of loving learning tend to develop a fixed mindset.

- They become more concerned with how they are being judged and fear that they might not live up to expectations.[64]

> **Growth Mindsets**

---

[64] Cherry, Kendra; What is a Mindset and Why Does it Matter; Very Well Mind; August 12, 2019; https://www.verywellmind.com/what-is-a-mindset-2795025

- Kids who are taught to explore, embrace new experiences, and enjoy challenges are more likely to develop a growth mindset.
- Rather than seeing mistakes as setbacks, they are willing to try new things and make errors all in the name of learning and achieving their potential.[65]

What is your mindset? Kendra Cherry, a psychosocial rehabilitation specialist, gives the following statements to determine which you are. Which do you agree with?

1. People have a certain amount of intelligence, and there isn't any way to change it.
2. No matter who you are, there isn't much you can do to improve your basic abilities and personality.
3. People are capable of changing who they are.
4. You can learn new things and improve your intelligence.

---
[65] See previous

5. People either have particular talents, or they don't. You can't just acquire talent for things like music, writing, art, or athletics.

6. Studying, working hard, and practicing new skills are all ways to develop new talents and abilities.

If you agree with statements 1, 2, and 5, then you probably have a fixed mindset. If you agree with 3, 4, and 6, you more than likely lean toward the growth mindset.

You have the power to change your thoughts and be successful. No one except you can take this away from you. Your success and is directly related to how you set your mind.

Chapter 11

Formidable Challenge

"I've missed more than 9000 shots in my career. I've lost almost 300 games. 26 times, I've been trusted to take the game winning shot and missed. I've failed over and over and over again in my life. And that is why I succeed."

- *Michael Jordan*

A Failure's True Power

Failure is an unfortunate fact of life. It isn't if it happens, it's when it happens. But you cannot have success if you don't have failure. Without it, we may not be as compassionate, empathetic; we may be less inclined to kindness or greater achievement. It is through failure that we learn the most valuable lessons in life.

For most, we think of failure in a negative way. It's painful and evokes the gamut of mental responses from guilt to remorse and everything in between. Indeed, it does hurt, but there are great gains. The simplest analogy would be that of a baby learning to walk. The baby is going to fall many times. These falls are failures. After many attempts, the baby will finally stand and walk. The balance was learned through the falls. The success gained through the lesson's failure taught.

Failure is, in fact, a steppingstone in life. There are five lessons that failure teaches us and helps to grant our successes.

1. Experience

The experience of failing at something is truly invaluable. It completely alters our frame-of-mind through the induction of pain. It makes us reflect on the real nature of things and their importance in our lives, transforming and improving our future-selves.

2. Knowledge

Failure brings important firsthand knowledge. That knowledge can be harnessed in the future to overcome that very failure that inflicted so much pain in the first place. Nothing can replace the knowledge gained from failure.

3. Resilience

Failing in life helps to build resilience. The more we fail, the more resilient we become.

In order to achieve great success, we must know resilience. Because, if we think that we're going to succeed on the first try or even the first few tries, then we're sure to set ourselves up for a far more painful failure.

4. Growth

When we fail, we grow and mature as human beings. We reach deeper meanings and understandings about our lives and why we're doing the things that we're doing. This helps us to reflect and take things into perspective, developing meaning from painful situations.

5. Value

One of the biggest lessons that we can learn from life's failures is the necessity to create and spread an exceedingly high amount of value. In fact, value lies at the heart of success, and a lack of value is a fundamental pillar to failure.[66]

"The difference between the novice and the master is that the master has failed more times than the novice has tried"

- *Koro Sensei (Yusei Matsui)*

Recovering from failure can be done if first we understand what failure is and that it's a necessary "evil" in our human experience. I'm not saying it's

---

[66] https://www.wanderlustworker.com/the-importance-of-failure-5-valuable-lessons-from-failing/

easy, only that it is doable. Here are some ways to help recover from failure.

- **Ignore the Naysayers**
  There's always going to be someone who says, "I told you so." Don't pay attention to them
- **Understand that it's Okay to Fail**
  It's really is ok to fail. Do a search on web; you'll find an infinite amount of failure stories even from the most successful of people.
- **Realize that it's Okay to Fail**
  Failure will take you on a journey that you might not want to go on. But, the reality of the situation is that those journeys will help to mold and shape you into a better person.
- **Using Failure as Leverage**
  Let failure push you into your future.
- **Revisit Your Goals**
  To recover from failure, revisit your goals and redefine them. Spend the time necessary to analyze and adjust where necessary.
- **Create a Massive Action Plan**
  Set out a solid action plan that will help you push past the stumbling blocks of life, and

watch as you slowly but surely recover from any setbacks, upsets, or failures.[67]

"The No. 1 reason people fail in life is because they listen to their friends, family, and neighbors."

- Napoleon Hill

It is so important, never to lose hope and always have the determination to bounce back through every trial and tribulation. Whether it be the loss of someone or a relationship you left, or if you became ill, continue to persevere. In these times, ask yourself these questions:

- How far can I go?
- What am I made of?
- Can I overcome or will I just quit like everybody else thinks I will?

Live to prove those that called you a failure wrong or give up and prove them right. People who fail focus on what they will have to go through; people who succeed focus on what it will feel like at the end. Dream of success yet endure failure when it happens. You can always take the easy way out, but Real strength comes when you decide to keep pushing forward no matter the circumstances.

---

[67] See previous

Struggle

Ironically, life with struggle is meaningful. Imagine watching a movie or TV shows where the main character wins every time without losing, training, learning or growing; it would not be satisfying. Rejoice in failures and losses for better days are coming. One day, when you truly overcome your struggle, you will notice how beautiful these times were as they built you and created who you are today.

Have you ever noticed just before the Olympic Games start, there's a pick-up in the businesses that train for those sports? No matter the sport, the gold medal fantasy comes to life. People are willing to struggle to achieve that greatness. Of course, Olympic Gold is elusive even for the highly trained athletes, so many who will try to achieve that goal probably wonder what got into them when they don't see immediate results. That's human.

The issue when we don't achieve what we've set out to do, or the road to that achievement is painful, is that we then feel inadequate. Those feelings may well come from our obsession of scoring the proverbial perfect 10, and when we don't, we feel like we've failed. That's ok.

Lea McLeod, a job and life coach based in New York City, offers these three suggestions when facing struggles:

1. Struggle is Not About Weakness
   It's easy to think that struggling with something is a sign of weakness; that if you're not good at math as a child, for example, you must not be very smart.

2. Struggle Fuels Growth
   Struggle is what happens in the gap between where you are and where you want to be. While it can be difficult and uncomfortable, this tension is where the real seeds of growth are planted.

3. Struggle Deepens Your Success
   Research indicates that the more you struggle and suffer setbacks while you're learning something new, the better you'll be able to recall and apply what you've learned in the future.[68]

---

[68] https://www.themuse.com/advice/how-your-struggles-can-get-you-to-the-top

> *"Who you are is defined by what you're willing to struggle for. People who enjoy the struggles of a gym are the ones who run triathlons and have chiseled abs and can bench-press a small house. People who enjoy long workweeks and the politics of the corporate ladder are the ones who fly to the top of it. People who enjoy the stresses and uncertainties of the starving artist lifestyle are ultimately the ones who live it and make it.*[69]
>
> *-   Mark Manson*

Be thankful for the struggles you go through. They make you stronger, wiser and humble. Don't let them break you. Let them make you.

Trust You're Struggle

The Urban Dictionary defines 'trust your struggle' as accepting when things are tough, it's for your benefit in the end; a life lesson that needs to be learned. Have you ever noticed that you run into the same types of problems or struggles? These are 'sticking' points that each of us has; struggles we continue to deny and resist.

Trusting those struggles, or sticking points, means that we stay awake and committed to the growth

---

[69] The Subtle Art of Not Giving a F*ck by Mark Manson ....
https://grahammann.net/book-notes/the-subtle-art-of-not-giving-a-fuck-mark-manson

required to move beyond the repetitive patterns that no longer suit us.[70]

The only way we can grow from our struggles is to really be in them, to understand the way we show up and our real intentions. If you can stay with the struggle instead of abandoning yourself or distracting yourself with substances, consumerism, media, or any other way of numbing out, you will be able to grow in ways you've probably needed to all of your life.

> *If you feel yourself hitting up against your limit, remember for what cause you to clench your fist. Remember why you started down this path, and let that memory carry you beyond your limit.*
>
> *- All Might (Kohei Horikoshi)*

Nothing in life is easy—there will always be hardships and obstacles to go through and it's the hard times that make us stronger. Struggles are required in order to survive in life because in order to stand up, you got to know what falling down is like.

---

[70] http://www.psychedinsanfrancisco.com/trust-struggle-mindfulness/

Identity Crisis

How you handle struggle will tell you a lot about who you are—how you think, behave, deal with situations—a crisis and even loss. But you can also become a victim of your situation if you feed it with negative thoughts.

If you feed into your 'struggle' by always mentioning your difficult dilemmas, then your struggle becomes your identity—how you see yourself and how others see you. This happens if you are emotionally stuck and can't move on from the situation.

> *"There are only two paths you can choose. You can sit quietly and be selected out of this world, or you can adapt and change!"*
>
> *- Gai Tsutsugami (Guilty Crown)*

Take something bad that happened in the past and see what positive came out of it. Think deep now. Did you become a stronger person, did you receive anything, did you learn a lesson, and did you meet a person because of this event? Even if it's dull, see the beauty in your struggle.

The beauties of those who endure through all their hardships and aim higher than the sky no longer seek validation as their accolades speak for themselves. Aim high, and you'll begin to see the hidden pictures in the canvas not clear to those who underestimate their capacity.

I leave you with this to ponder, what are you willing to struggle for?

Cruise Control

Fearing or not wanting to 'deal' with struggle can lead to complacency. You're not necessarily happy with where you are, but it works, it's easy, and you're cruising along just fine. You're on autopilot. In this mode, we don't see that the meaning of life is, in part, our struggles. Struggling in reaching a worthy goal grants fulfillment. Life doesn't have to be mundane—same thing only different day—it can be full of wonderful experiences. However, if you are happy in this mode, then disregard this paragraph. But...

When you get comfortable and complacent, eventually, life catches up to you. Some event will occur, forcing you to change. If you continue to grow and further expand your horizon, then life will not have to force you to change as you are changing on your own. I'll give you an example. You start a new job, you're upbeat, and everything is going well. Your work is good, your coworkers are friendly, and you couldn't be happier. Now fast forward 10 months; you're showing up late, not caring too much about your appearance, maybe coming in unshaven or with no makeup. Your work IS still good, but not as good as it was when you first started. You continue this process, and now your employer has decided to let you go. You got comfortable, became complacent, and the path you took was not a path that made you better, so you needed a change. Another example is when a superstar gets traded. They were comfortable and not working as hard, but being traded woke them up and gave them a new motivation. They were no longer in their comfort zone as they were in their grind one now, which in all makes players have some of the best seasons they have ever had. It's ok to be comfortable, but you must stay motivated and have the discipline and determination to keep excelling.

> *"A comfort zone is a beautiful place, but nothing ever grows there."*
>
> *Unknown*

A lot of times we get comfortable in our jobs because we know the people and how to do our job. Don't become too comfortable because there could be better opportunities for you. the grind should be even better during your time of comfort. Keep striving for more. It's hard to stay at the top because when things are going well, we get comfortable while there is somebody who is working twice as hard, slowly catching up day by day. Don't waste each day; have the same attitude as if you're going to your first job interview.

Life has levels like a video game. We don't ask why when things are going well until something bad happens. Maybe it's because we have already beaten this level of life, so if we don't go to the next level on our own, life will force us there. By 'next level,' I mean to continue to grow, which means doing something that will aid in you being a smarter and better person. We get comfortable as if we are playing a level in a game that we have already beaten. Sometimes, we reach a level we can't win, so we have to restart and go over the basics. When you reach a point in life where you have to restart, look at it as: *if I was to continue, then I would not beat the game now. I'm given a chance to redo things and beat the game.* The game ends when we are no longer awake in this world, so keep playing until that day comes.

Get out of your comfort zone. Don't get complacent. You can be better. Always strive for more until you can't strive anymore.

Follower or Leader?

Most people follow the crowd as it is more comfortable. Have the courage to go with what you feel and not the flock. It's interesting that if a professor puts a question up and asks you to raise your hand on which answer you believe. You are more likely to raise your hand on the answer when everybody else does. Don't follow the crowd all the time, have the confidence in your own intellect.

> *"A leader takes people where they want to go. A great leader takes people where they don't necessarily want to go, but ought to be"*
>
> *-   Rosalynn Carter*

If you feel like your purpose is to be a leader, then understand what that entails. Being a leader means not only getting you out of the fire but others as well. It is hard enough dealing with our own problems, but when you are a leader, you must help others deal with theirs. They look up to you, and you may be the only light they have in their life. Now, if you give up on them, they may give up on themselves. It's not that they are dependent on you, but as a leader, you might have the power to make or break someone. Yet do not let helping others destroy yourself as it is useless to assist others while killing you from within.

Being a leader can be frustrating at times, but you must remain strong. If you lose focus, the probability is very high that others will lose focus too.

Understand your true potential, just because others you know may be doing "better" than you, don't think of yourself as a follower. Think of yourself as a leader because there are others watching and who look up to you; trust me. It might not be visible, but people do. Even the greatest leaders have looked up to someone. We all have a leader in us; it just takes the right mindset and experiences to bring it out, in my opinion. Understand why you do things, not why things happen. We have control over why we do the things we do but not over why sometimes.

A leader isn't someone who has followers to me, but someone who can bring out the best in others and then utilize those strengths to form an even greater team and increase the output of success.

Art of Adversity

> *"The flower that blooms in adversity is the most rare and beautiful of all."*
>
> *- Mulan (Robert D. San Souci)*

Adversity is a state or instance of serious or continued difficulty or misfortune. While synonymous with 'struggle' in terms of it being a difficulty, and we've already discussed it above, I wanted to add five points to help you overcome it here.

1. Be aware of, and accept that adversity is inevitable in life. Adversity is part of life. To avoid or resist it will only make it persist.
2. Build your internal resources. Before adversity hits, work on building emotional strength, courage and discipline.

3. Build your external resources. Build a support system of family and friends. When the going gets tough, we all need encouragement and support.
4. That which does not kill you doesn't *always* make you stronger. This statement differs from Nietzsche, where he says, "that what does not kill you will make you stronger." If you don't build up your resilience, then adversity can absolutely crush you. How? Think of resilience like a muscle. Muscles are built up over time and especially with continued exposure to different obstacles

5. Take inspiration and learn from others who have dealt successfully with adversity. There are many notable people who've over tremendous odds and went on to live successful, productive lives rather than surrender to the adversity. Here is a short list of some of them.

   a. **J.K. Rowling:** Born to a poor family; left a bad marriage with a young baby to live on government assistance; wrote her first Harry Potter book and was turned down by most publishers until Bloomsbury Publishing picked it up.[71]

b. **Helen Keller:** Lost her sight and hearing due to a mysterious fever when she was only 18 months old. She overcame her deafness and blindness to become a strong, educated woman who promoted women's rights.[72]

c. **Temple Grandin**: Born with autism and had a lot of difficulty in her early school days. Little was known about the autism spectrum in the late 40s. She went on to earn her Ph.D. in animal husbandry and is now a professor of animal science and an activist for autism rights.

d. **Andres Galarraga**: One-time pitcher of the Atlanta Braves, diagnosed with non-Hodgkin's Lymphoma in 1999. After being treated, he returned to the game in 2000. That year his batting average was .302, he hit 28 home runs and 100 RBI. This was good enough to

---

[71] https://www.essentiallifeskills.net/overcoming-adversity.html
[72] https://www.essentiallifeskills.net/overcoming-adversity.html

earn him a comeback player of the year award.[73]

e. **Eric Davis**: During the 1997 season, Davis was diagnosed with colon cancer. His diagnosis was met with an unlikely promise: Davis vowed to return that same season. And return he did.

In 1998, Davis had the fourth best batting average in the league and strung together a 30-game hitting streak. Pretty impressive for a guy who was one year removed from cancer.[74]

If you really want something, you'll do whatever it takes to make it happen. Whatever the challenge or adversity is, stick to it—see it through. Keep in mind to be moral, ethical, and legal about accomplishing your goal. It may take 5, 10, 20 years, but you have to keep moving forward. Like the people named above, things might seem dull and hopeless, but for every dark day, a brighter one will shine as long as you keep your faith and hope alive.

---

[73] https://bleacherreport.com/articles/429073-fighting-back-15-athletes-who-have-battled-adversity#slide10
[74] https://bleacherreport.com/articles/429073-fighting-back-15-athletes-who-have-battled-adversity#slide10

Chapter 12

Resolve

If something is perfect, then there is nothing left. There is no room for imagination. No place left for that person to gain additional knowledge or abilities. Do you know what that means? For scientists such as us, perfection only brings despair. It is our job to create things more wonderful than anything before them, but never to obtain perfection. A scientist must be a person who finds ecstasy while suffering from that antinomy.
- *Kurotsuchi Mayuri (Tite Kubo)*

Mission Success

We've talked about how to find your path but not why. Regardless of what path we choose, ultimately, we want to be successful. Success doesn't come easy—it comes with hard work, dedication, and sometimes sacrifices. It's a combination of failures, mistakes, and setbacks. It's ultimately a reward at the end of a journey riddled with challenges that weed out the weak and unmotivated.

It is unlikely that your path through life will match the exact journey you had in mind when you set out. It makes no sense to restrict your satisfaction to one scenario when there are many paths to success.

Everything we've talked about leads us here. But how do we achieve success, and what does success mean? Is it happiness, wealth, power? Miriam-Webster's defines success as a: degree or measure of succeeding b: favorable or desired outcome it is also the attainment of wealth, favor, or eminence.[75]

Zig Ziglar was a modern-day expert on success. He argued that success couldn't be defined in one sentence, but instead, it is comprised of many things.[76] The meaning of success is person-specific if you will. We all have a different perception of success. Here are a few definitions. Which one(s) apply to you?

> Success is always doing your best
> Success is properly setting concrete goals
> Success is having a place to call home
> Success is understanding the difference between need and want
> Success is believing you can
> Success is remembering to balance work with passion
> Success is taking care of your needs
> Success is learning that you sometimes have to say no

---

[75] https://www.merriam-webster.com/dictionary/success
[76] Ziglar, Zig; Born to Win; January 2012; Made for Success Publishing; Seattle, WA

- > Success is knowing your life is filled with abundance
- > Success is understanding you cannot keep what you don't give away
- > Success is overcoming fear
- > Success is learning something new each day
- > Success is learning that losing a few battles can help you win a war
- > Success is loving and being loved back
- > Success is standing your ground when you believe in something
- > Success is celebrating small victories
- > Success is never letting a disability hold you back
- > Success is understanding you control your destiny

Looks simple right? Not! There's nothing easy about success, even if we know what we want. It's getting there. The truth is, success requires a lot of hard work. Then, what is the secret to success? How did people like Kenneth Frazier, Oprah Winfrey, or Robert L. Johnson achieve success? More than likely, they figured out how to work smart. They understand how to schedule their priorities rather than prioritize their schedule. They also understand the secrets of willpower, manage their stress, and nurture their relationships.[77]

"Success is liking yourself, liking what you do, and liking how you do it."

- Maya Angelou

There are many ways to work smarter, but first, we have to look at the reasons we don't. We live in an age where we are constantly distracted, whether it be text messages, phone calls, internet—we are constantly connected, which doesn't give us time to think through our thoughts. We can achieve what successful people have by implementing the following mindsets.

> Decide What's Most Important
>> o Because of the constant demands on our time, it's difficult to get everything done we need to. We need to be clear about our priorities, have a vision as to where we are going, and be committed to our goals.
> Be Accountable

---

[77] https://www.psychologytoday.com/us/blog/the-mindful-self-express/201311/what-truly-successful-people-know-you-dont

- Don't just set goals, keep track of your progress, and create incentives for yourself.
> Confront Mindlessness
- It's easy to allow our thoughts to drift away from the task at hand, especially if we are sick, tired, or very stressed. When you find yourself drifting, remind yourself to go back to the task. Successful people remind themselves several times a day to be mindful.
> Set Boundaries and say "No"
- Don't overbook yourself and agree to do things you don't have time or care to do. Successful people know that you have to give up some opportunities and potential rewards to honor your commitment to your highest priorities
> Build Supportive Relationships
- We are human and one of our basic needs, as discussed in Chapter 2, is the need for connection. We need the support of others to keep going and help us weather the disappointments on the path to success. Successful people

know that doing it alone can only take you so far.
> Make Time to Replenish Yourself
  o You need to take time to rest and relax. Maintaining a high level of performance over long periods can wear down our willpower. We can't help looking out for others if we don't look out after ourselves first.

Dr. Melanie Greenburg has done a lot of research on the secrets of success. The six points above are some of the results of her extensive work.[78]

Success isn't easy to attain; we have to work for it. No one can hand us success on a silver platter; it doesn't work that way. In life, we're all dealt a hand with pleasure and hardship. I believe that we are given exactly what it is we need to learn to become our better selves.

> *"Success is going from failure to failure without losing your enthusiasm."*
>
> *- Winston Churchill*

Most successful people will tell you that it took a lot of hard work to get where they are. Ironically,

---

[78] https://www.psychologytoday.com/us/blog/the-mindful-self-express/201311/what-truly-successful-people-know-you-dont

the psychology of success is often overlooked. It does take hard work, but that's only part of it. You must also have the right mindset.

Your mindset will determine your success. Remember, if you listen to your mind when its focused-on negativity, telling you that you're a failure, then you will be. If you listen to your mind when it tells you you're on the right track and keep going, then you will have a far better chance at succeeding. Which voice will you listen to?

There are many successful people. David Goggins is someone I admire and follow. David Goggins is a retired Navy Seal and an ultra-endurance athlete who has run some of the toughest races in the world. He believes that you do what you want to do and keep doing it. He had a lot of low points in his life, but never let that deter him. Mr. Goggins thrived on overcoming challenges and adversity. He understood that with each challenge he met and beat, it made him mentally stronger.

So, then how do we gain a successful mentality? Joyce Marter,[79] a psychotherapist, life-coach, has broken it down for us. Here are a few steps to help.

---

[79] Joyce Marter, LCPC is a licensed psychotherapist and Founder of Urban Balance, a counseling private practice with over 100 therapists

1. **Become conscious of why you do what you do.** We all come into our careers or life situations for a reason. If things aren't working the way you believe they should look at your behaviors. Are you holding onto something that isn't working anymore? Give yourself permission to let go of those behaviors.
2. **Open yourself up to prosperity.** Try to constrain yourself with self-limiting beliefs. As Dr. Joyce Brothers said, "Success is a state of mind. If you want success, start thinking of yourself as a success."
3. **Bring your attention to the present.** Honor the past, learn from it, and let it go. Don't obsess or worry about the future. Discover the power of mindfulness practices such as deep

---

working from eight locations in Chicagoland & St. Louis. Marter received her Masters Degree in Counseling Psychology from Northwestern University and was awarded Distinguished Alumni of the Year in 2008. She was selected by Crain's Chicago Business for the "40 Under 40" List of 2010. She currently serves as the Chair-Elect of the Midwest Region of the American Counseling Association, is Past-President of the Illinois Counseling Association, and is two-term Past-President of the Illinois Mental Health Counselors Association. Marter is a blogger for PsychCentral on The Psychology of Success. She has a passion for applying psychology to business and is a public speaker for corporations, universities and professional organizations. Marter is routinely consulted as a psychological expert on television, radio and has been featured in such publications as The Wall Street Journal, U.S. News & World Report and MTV.

breathing and meditation, which keep you firmly grounded in the present moment.

4. **Discover the power of intention.** Wayne Dyer says, "Our intentions create our reality." Identify your intentions, write them out, and live by them.

5. **Develop your vision.** As in sports psychology, positive visualization increases the likelihood of success. Ask yourself, if you had a magic wand, what would you want? Aim high. Look for how your strengths and gifts can benefit others, creating a "win-win" scenario.

6. **Silence your inner critic.** Pay attention to your self-talk and notice if you have negative thoughts rooted in the past. Separate from negative beliefs by "zooming out" and looking at situations from an objective and neutral place.

7. **Practice positive thinking.** Understand that positivity attracts positivity through the laws of attraction. Keep a gratitude journal. Choose to be your best cheerleader rather than your worst critic.

8. **Practice acceptance.** Don't expend energy fighting or resisting what you cannot change

(other people, their feelings, their behaviors, etc.). Instead, empower yourself to change what you can (your thinking, your behaviors, your boundaries, etc.). If for no other reason than to free you, forgive and let go of resentments.

9. **Appreciate that personal and professional progress is not linear.** We all go through setbacks. It's how we respond to those setbacks that determine if we are going to endlessly cycle or stagnate or grow and develop. Cut yourself some slack and recognize we are all human and are works in progress. Learn from mistakes, be resilient and forge ahead.

10. **Love yourself.** Practice self-compassion and self-care. Establish work/life balance and a positive support network for yourself. Demonstrate this self-love by making a commitment to achieving your greatest successes in life.[80]

---

[80] https://www.huffpost.com/entry/the-psychology-of-success_b_4306761

> *"The first step toward success is taken when you refuse to be a captive of the environment in which you first find yourself."*
>
> \- *Mark Caine*

Your mindset could be the one factor keeping you from becoming successful. If you put the harder tasks off until later, eventually, there won't be a later. The day will arrive when you will have needed to complete those tasks, including changing your mindset, and you will find yourself without the tools you need to succeed. Focus on what you can do today. If you have been putting things off, ask yourself why and what are you doing to change that. Only then you can create your success.

If having a family or working a job is your reason for not achieving success, then why do these barriers only stop the majority and not everybody? If it were easy, then everybody would attempt, which is why success is rare depending on how you define it. You can continue on as you are or live to defy the odds stacked up against you like how Vince Carter has been playing in the NBA for 22 years.

Now that you know the secrets of successful people, take the time to look at yourself. Have the courage to be honest with you. You can be successful—start with your personal habits today.

Most Valuable Player

In society, success isn't about self-contentment or the path to fulfillment. It is more about how the world perceives you, how people think of you, and how others would look up to you. Success takes a little bit of luck plus hardship, but when you are rewarded the benefits of success, you can easily lose yourself to your new image.

When you become engulfed in success, as you are willing to do anything in order to bring the life you envision to fruition, you can lose out on key elements along your journey. You may even begin to neglect not only vital parts of your life but the core of your inner self as well. This neglect can lead to hindering you from becoming whole and immaculate in your field of endeavor. Such a person whose eyes are on the prize will inevitably find the success he wishes for but will see how empty this achievement may feel as it doesn't fulfill the void that they desired to be satisfied.

So, if success is one of the final destinations of our journey, how could it be bad to focus only on success? Time after time we see an induvial who achieves success yet for all the wrong reasons. Some will achieve success in hope that what they dreamed would bring them happiness or power but quite the contrary. Now don't get me wrong success is not bad but the temptation that comes with it makes it easy to lose sight of who you are which is my main argument. The trick is to elevate your core values as you'll end up with double. A magnanimous person plus success is what yields when you chase becoming a person of value which in my eyes is a pretty damn good combination

The person with limitless core values understands his worth and not that materialistic things or the people he hangs around define them. Think of it like a value meal so to speak. The more quality food that comes with the meal, the better value it has. Quality over quantity. You don't need to be a person of a million values but the gift you bring to life could be the only value you need. One value could branch off to others with one core value being the mother tree. Another example is in basketball, you have guys who shoot threes only, are only great defenders, are only good passers, are only rebounders and dunkers the list goes on. The playstyle is what is of value. Some teams need a three-point shooter so because of the value he brings, it has brought him success as he signs a new contract. Yet there are some players who can do it all which is why their value is so imperative like Michael Jordan, Kobe Bryant and Lebron James.

The person of value doesn't fall prey to what the majority is easily swayed by. They realize that to be content with themselves and be satisfied with life, that they must genuinely be grateful and appreciative for all aspects of life. They must be able to comprehend their strengths and weaknesses as they know what weaknesses they can transform into strengths and what weaknesses are who they are, which are things that can't be changed by hard work like trying to grow in height. This nirvana will catapult such a person to be able to overcome his many flaws and better upgrade his worthiness to society. This person is a person of great virtue, and therefore, great value.

James Hurford, DTM offers these 8 steps to become a person of value:

1. **Find your purpose and passion**
   The great and influential men and women the world has ever known where those who

discovered and pursued their purpose and were driven by their passions.

When you're on the path of purpose, it's easier to add significant value to the lives of others. You'll hardly be of any significant value to people or influence them when you don't know where you are going yourself.

Purpose ignites passion which keeps you motivated, inspired and focused. You need that to be valuable and influential.

2. **Embrace personal development**

   Becoming a person of value and influence demands embracing a lifelong pursuit of personal development. Personal development is a process of understanding and developing yourself to realize your full potential.

   The extent to which you're able to add value and influence others depends on the extent to which you have been able to develop yourself. Every raw material has little or no value. It becomes valuable after its been refined. Take time to refine yourself in every area. That could be hard but it's rewarding. Daily ask yourself, "What do I need to learn or do to become a better person?

   Your value depends on the value you offer.

3. **Choose a problem you can solve for people**

   To be a person of value and influence, you have to become genuinely interested in people enough to solve a specific problem for them. Think of what you can do to make lives better. The more people you solve problems for, the more valuable and influential you become.

4. **Be original and unique**

   When we live our lives mimicking or imitating others, it steals our originality. Guess what? Imitations don't get much attention, originals do. We've all heard that when you imitate someone else, the best you can be is second best. That's very true. To be a person of influence doesn't be anyone else. Be YOU.

5. **Pursue excellence**

   Becoming a person of value and influence is not going to be so much about what you do as it is about how well you do it. It's said that whatever is worth doing is worth doing well. Go beyond the usual. Add a touch of class in all you do. That's what excellence is all about. Mind you it's not the same as perfection.

6. **Encourage and inspire others**

   Find a way to encourage and inspire others to be all they can be. Empower, share your knowledge and skills with others. Your value and influence is connected to the number of lives that are better because of you.

7. **Exude confidence**

   Self-confidence is one quality that's very admirable. It's about knowing what you want and having the courage and boldness to go for it. When you're self-confident, people are attracted to you. When you don't have it, the opposite is the case. The reason is simple—what value do you think a person who doesn't believe in himself offers?

8. **Have integrity**

    It's true that none of us is perfect but for you to be a person of value and influence you have to be able to earn people's confidence and trust. You should be able to live by certain values that uphold sound moral principles.

    Integrity means doing the right thing at all times and in all circumstances, whether or not it's convenient. It's about being sincere and real. It's about being honest enough to admit when you're wrong. It's your "yes" as "yes" and your "no" as "no". It's people trusting you not for any other reason but because you have earned their trust. [81]

Success and value should go hand and hand. Strive for success but in doing so aim to become of value. The more valuable you are the better off you will be. The more successful you become the easier it is to

---

[81] https://www.linkedin.com/pulse/how-become-person-value-influence-james-hurford/

fall prey to that forbidden fruit. A level of equality should be the goal between the two. I want you though to keep in mind that adding value to yourself is more difficult, which is why Albert Einstein's quote is a good reminder to ensure that you are striving to help others in the grand scheme of your life! Which I personally think should be practiced by all.

"Strive not to be a success, but rather to be of value."

- Albert Einstein

Part IV

Humanitarian

X

Highlight

Chapter 13

Engulfed in Entitlement

"It is impossible to escape the impression that people commonly used false standards of measurement- that they seek power, success and wealth for themselves and admires them in others, and that they underestimate what is of true value."

- Sigmund Freud

Greed Island

Take away our status, money, job title, materialistic things, and we are all the same, nothing less nothing more. Don't let your accolades or experiences make you forget that.

Money can give you power. There are those who have enough in which they can do anything. Money can make you feel more entitled than others; it can create a sense of arrogance. When you become arrogant, you begin to feel untouchable, and when you feel untouchable, bad things are bound to catch up to you. Be thankful for your accolades as it is a representation of your hard work. Remain humble. My point is never to forget where you come from.

Don't become greedy when you succeed. Don't let the shadow of greed overcome yourself. Greed really is out there. Don't succumb to it because you may lose everything.

The money keeps us caged. We are dependent and only act when money is involved. We do things for money. We buy things for how expensive they are. The more you think about money, the bigger your avarice. Now, by all means, don't be poor but aim to be wealthy in compassion and not only riches. Money doesn't buy happiness as it is too expensive, but what you do with that money can create happiness.

Power

For centuries, power has been defined by Machiavelli's *"The Prince."* This book, written over 500 years ago, advocates the  politics of necessity and the need to achieve a balance of force, fear ad guile. One of Machiavelli's most famous lines is: "... in the actions of men, and especially of princes, the end justifies the means." The book's influence is so great that the adjective

'Machiavellian' is used to describe amoral, scheming, and duplicitous behavior.[82]

We have followed Machiavelli's advice for centuries. We have come to believe that we can only gain power through deception, manipulation, force, coercion, and fear. We assume to be in a position of power we need to be cold and calculating.

These ideas, though sadly seductive, are wrong on every level. A new science of power has shown that in order for power to wield effectively, it must be used intelligently with empathy and social intelligence. The days of reigns of terror should be kept in history.

While current research debunks the Machiavellian power myths, studies have also shown that once people come into positions of power, they are more prone to act impulsive and aggressive. They sometimes have a difficult time seeing the world as others do, which creates the power paradox.[83] Meaning, the skills that we need to obtain power and lead are those that we lose once in power.

---

[82] https://www.italymagazine.com/featured-story/machiavellis-prince-ultimate-guide-power

[83] Keltner, Dachar Ph.D.; The Power Paradox: How We Gain and Lose Influence; Penguin Books; NY, NY; May 2017;

Power is a strange animal. Some of the most powerful and influential leaders have created catastrophic results with its misuse. Extreme examples would be Adolf Hitler and Jimmy Jones. Leaders, or those in powerful places, are able to evoke change and influence people. It is critical that we strive for the greater good when we are in positions of power.

> *"Hitler and Mussolini were only the primary spokesmen for the attitude of domination and craving for power that are in the heart of almost everyone. Until the source is cleared, there will always be confusion and hate, wars and class antagonisms"*
>
> *- Jiddu Krishnamurti*

Do not become consumed by power, it will turn you into an arriviste crappy person. Only achieving power will be on your mind and anything else that doesn't relate to that or help that will become annoying to you, thus, you will mistreat it.

Lord Acton wrote that "power tends to corrupt." Research has concluded that power does come with temptation and that power "tends to corrupt." It doesn't have to. There are four science-based strategies to help you use your power ethically.

1. Focus on the responsibility that comes with power
    a. Set your expectations based on your ideas and values, not what everyone else is thinking?
2. Develop a strong moral identity
    a. Someone with a strong sense of morality, someone who sees caring, generosity, and justice a core part of who they are, are not as likely to be self-focused when they receive power.
3. Encourage others to voice
    a. Solicit other people's opinions. Give them a voice. Share the power and encourage people to speak up.
4. Find mentors to keep you humble
    a. Find an honest who can offer support and pop your power bubble by giving you honest feedback about your behavior.

Seeking power is the downfall to a lot of people because they desire it for the wrong reasons. Your reason should be to protect what's precious to you. Yet we abuse it. Some want it because they feel entitled because of where they come from. Some want it for their own egos. Some want it in order to get back to those who wronged them. Seek power in order to make a change and help out others. When you seek power for another reason, it can transform you into a person your kid self would have never thought you would become. Realize what's important in life, and that's doing the best I can, achieving my highest self and helping out as many people as I can.

When you have power, you become arrogant and also alienated. You may think that you're invincible but do not take life for granted, as your life can change in the blink of an eye. Remind yourself that this very moment is the only one you know you have for sure. Be grateful for what you have because life can change in a second. Be humble and stay true to yourself, no matter your status. Treat others the way you want to be treated, not how they treat you.

<u>Genuine Humility</u>

A study conducted by the University of Washington Foster School of Business found that "humble people tend to make the most effective leaders and are more likely to be high performers in both individual and team settings."[84]

---

[84] https://www.entrepreneur.com/article/238328

Humility, many times, is confused with low self-esteem. The truth is it isn't thinking less *of* yourself but rather less *about* yourself. True humility encompasses perceptiveness, kindness, and yes, self-awareness. It makes you more honest, kinder, and more giving.

To be a truly effective leader, you need to be honest about your strengths and shortcomings. You can be confident without being conceited, supportive without submission, and certainly open-minded without abstinence.

A humble person asks for feedback from family, friends, and co-workers. This can go a long way to boost morale in a company, help you set realistic goals, and significantly increase your chance at an earlier rather than later success.

Stephen Covey, in his book, "The 7 Habits of Highly Effective People," wrote: "A humble person is more concerned about what is right than about being right. About acting on good ideas than having good ideas. About embracing new truth than depending on outdated position. About building the team than exalting self, about recognizing contribution, then being recognized."

Humility is difficult to maintain, especially as you climb through life. The example would be someone who drives a high-end car. If you watch them on the road, there's a sense of entitlement that seems to come with that car. Suddenly the rules don't apply to them. They can drive in the emergency lane on the freeways, not stop at a stop sign, and even make left-hand turns in front of you. It's not a lot different as we reach our higher goals. We've worked to get there, so, therefore, we're entitled to more.

- HUMILITY KEEPS YOU FOCUSED
    - Humility keeps you focused on the things that matter.
        - A smile
        - A touch
        - A warm meal
        - Love
- HUMILITY KEEPS YOU TEACHABLE
Through humility, we are always reminded that there may be someone behind us, but most certainly, someone is always ahead of us, regardless of our success.
- HUMILITY KEEPS YOU HAPPY

- When you embrace humility, you are reminded that everything you have is a blessing.

For your last Mission, I challenge you to donate or volunteer to five things before you start your next TV show series or leisure activity.

You may also as an option help at least one person you know who really needs help. Show them that there are compassionate people who do good deeds out of the kindness of their heart

Remember don't lose yourself to your attachments. Remain humble—you'll go a lot further in life.

Chapter 14
Eyes of the Immortal

"When do you think people die? When they are shot through the heart by the bullet of a pistol? No. When they are ravaged by an incurable disease? No. when they drink a soup made from a poisonous mushroom!? No! It's when...they are forgotten"

– Dr. Hiriluk (Eiichiro Oda)

An Immortal Legacy

We are truly gone when we are forgotten as our gift, art, ideals, or impact may live forever.

Life is like the wind—it comes and goes. A lot of us start to plan our lives as kids, whether that's to be a musician, a sports star, or a famous actor and the list goes on. We want to be great, perhaps like baseball player Mike Trout who recently signed a contract with the Los Angeles Angels for 430 million dollars or maybe the queen Beyoncé, whose net worth is estimated to be 355 million dollars.

Society encourages us to be the most popular and that money is the key to all success. If we don't have fame or fortune, can we live a life to be remembered? Of course, we can. There are some simple philosophies we need to employ.

> Leave a Legacy to emulate
> Serve magnanimously, giving more than you take
> If you happen to live to be remembered, it becomes timeless and unforgettable.

"Love is how you stay alive, even after you are gone"
- *Mitch Albom*

We have the power to have a positive impact on life. Sadly, we are so pre-occupied with our own daily lives we forget how we affect others or to make our lives rewarding. With our time here on earth, we want people to think of the good things we've done.

Remember, it's not how long you live, but what difference you made while being alive as a thing isn't beautiful because it lasts forever. There are a lot of people in their graves who have lived a hundred years and have never started their real journey.

Coda

Lift Off

You may have found yourself feeling like you were reading some of the same points over and over again. Interesting, isn't it? I wasn't trying to be redundant, yet a piece to a puzzle is still a piece of many pieces. No matter what part of ourselves we are trying to change to be the best us we can be, there are some basic tenets.

> Honesty
> Kindness
> Charity
> Integrity
> Selflessness

I'm not saying it's easy. In fact, I've pointed out that choosing our path and walking our journey is not always a paved road—there will be bumps, bruises, and scrapes along the way. It's how we choose our path and walk our walk that will make the difference.

When we create a positive change within ourselves, our image changes. A new image brings new hope, and the cycle continues. The problem is that we stop moving as if it were at a permanent stop sign. If we don't persevere through tough times, then a list of traumas can occur. We must release ourselves, our spirit, our mind from the hands of time, and flow with the time we are allocated on earth. Walk a path that you cherish every day, no matter what others think. Those who truly respect and appreciate you will understand and have nothing but best wishes. Don't give up on those who would discourage you, as change, to some, is difficult, but with time they may come around. Time heals everything as long as you believe in what you are going through, who you are, and what you wish to accomplish is all according to your divine plan.

> *"You should enjoy the little detours. To the fullest. Because that's where you'll find the things more important than what you want"*
>
> - *Ging Freecs (Yoshihiro Togashi)*

You have only one life. Live it up. Matter of fact, make a bucket list of things to do right now before you pass away, and see what it is you can get done. You want to feel bliss when your time comes. A life where you worked hard, failed, succeeded, loved, lost, gained, laughed, and smiled. A life where you had so much fun and helped so many people, you are content. That life can be for anybody no matter where you come from or where you are at with your life. A short-lived life doing things you love is better than a long-lived life doings thing you dread.

Remember these seven points as you go through your journey. These will help guide you along the path.

1. Everything happens for a reason.
2. There's no failure, only feedback.
3. Whatever happens, take responsibility?
4. It is not necessary to understand everything to use everything.
5. People are your greatest resource.
6. Work is play.
7. There's no abiding success without commitment.

In Chapter 1, I asked you to answer 12 questions. Answer them again and see if any of your answers have changed. More than likely, some have. Remember, there are no right or wrong answers, only truthful ones.

- What attachments can't I let go of and can I live without these earthly attachments?
- What is out there that you would jeopardize your life to protect?
- Do you still harbor guilt from any event in your life, if so, why?
- What is my purpose or reason for being in this world?
- What illusions do I continue to uphold, and why?
- What are some of the lies that I tell myself?
- What grief have I not been able to forgive?
- What would others say at my funeral?
- What are you ashamed of, and why?
- What are you most afraid of?
- What are my core values?
- What do I hate?

Use the lessons in this book as a guideline. I know they worked for me, and they still do. Remember that we have to be able to look at that reflection in the mirror and be happy with who we see.

Never forget your path is not an end destination, but a journey with adverse challenges requiring constant perseverance, faith, and to consciously make a decision that you deserve better each and every day.

Write your own Notes

Acknowledgments

There have been many individuals throughout my life who have helped me and I would like to acknowledge a few of them.

As I believe in **GOD**, I would like to thank Him for all the blessings He has given me—the good and the bad.

My unique **Family.** To my beautiful mother who has always believed in me and given me the courage to chase my dreams. To my father who has supported me from day one and always worked in my best interest. To my older sisters who set a great foundation for me while growing up. Also, to my cousin Chidi, who told me when I wanted to give up, "what if your kids go through this exact moment and they ask what you did, do you want to tell them you gave up or persevered?" That question made me grind even harder when I was losing hope. Thank you.

Shout out to the animes **Naruto, One Piece, and YuYu Hakausho** for teaching me more about myself than grade school ever did and also for giving me an awesome thrill as to continuously wonder what happens next for years. Anime isn't just a cartoon; it's full of good fights and life lessons that you never could fathom. These animes influenced me in so many ways. Most people don't know the knowledge of anime but by reading this I hope you got a sample. Masashi Kishimoto, Eiichiro Oda and Yoshihiro Togashi, thank you for changing my life.

Lori Stewart, who teaches Religious Studies and psychology classes at San Diego State, changed my view of life—she woke me up. She made me realize so much about myself and gave me so much insight which led me into who I am today. The knowledge she bestowed upon me helped steer me into a direction I'm so happy to be walking. Thank you.

Brad Kirkegaard, who shared a quote I will forever live by: "Life is what you make of it." Your benevolence was so contagious it made me want to be just as happy for life as you are. Thank you.

Estralita Martin made me think about my life in a different way. I'm not sure if I ever truly reciprocated, but she still went out of her way for me. It never went unappreciated. Thank you.

Thelma Chavez, who helped me during my college years, showing me that we all need a little help sometimes, Thank you.

Eric Thomas - Your speech, "How Bad Do You Want It," changed my life and made me want to become the best version of myself. Thank you.

Last but not least I would like to thank **Liane Larocque** for turning my notes into the book that you have decoded. It was her expertise and brilliance that made my thoughts flow nicely. We all need help in this world, and I would not have completed this book without her. Liane's great intellect and passion for writing is the best I have seen in a long time. Look into her other work as it won't let you down.

Week Paid Vacation

Back in the day during school, when the teacher wasn't looking, my friends and I would play basketball by shooting a crumpled piece of paper into the recycling bin. The playful competition and the thrill of the teacher not noticing made it that much better, or maybe the teacher didn't care as kids were being kids. Even in offices, you can find mini basketball hoops, as such a simple game makes you feel like a kid again. I preach to never lose that innocence within you, so I propose a mini-game for you. I challenge you to crumple up 5 pieces of paper that you don't care about or can dispose of and shoot all 5 into a trash can similar to shooting a basketball into a hoop and see who can make the most between you and some friends. You are allowed only 2 off the wall shots. I need proof of who won, so I want you to post a video of the contest and tag me on Instagram (jalbritton52) with the hash tag, #Neverloseyourinnocence. I want to start a movement that brings a smile to peoples face and what better way then by playing a game that brought some of us bliss as kids. The person who generates the most likes, I'll personally invite them on my first trip during my book tour. Just envision a week paid vacation if you need the motivation. My aim is too conglomerate my readers as they can see just how not alone, they are. The responsibilities and calamities of life can make us lose that inner child. I want to reignite that feeling, and the only way I know how is by having fun. This innocence could be a beacon of light that we unknowingly may need to shine on us ever so vibrantly.

Authors Short Story

I remember it like it was yesterday. It was my last year of college at San Diego State. I was in great athletic shape, ready to play Division 1 basketball as a walk-on during the Steve Fisher era. I was finally going to finish my engineering degree. I had a great girlfriend. I was studying for my Engineering in training certificate. I lived in a two-bedroom apt with my own room, which overlooked almost the entire city from my balcony. Things were going great, and I couldn't be happier, but in the matter of a few months, I would almost lose everything, including myself. But let's rewind a little bit to my freshmen year.

When I moved into the dorms my freshmen year, it was an awesome feeling. Being on my own for a change brought so much euphoria. No more rules but more responsibilities, yet I was ready to tackle college. I saw how the basketball players were treated, and I wanted that swag plus notoriety. To go from a small high school averaging 20 points a game to a top 25 college basketball school made my ego jump for joy. It fueled my motivation to train even harder. Fast forward a little, and tryouts were here. When I tried out, I played great, actually I scored the most during the scrimmages but not to my luck, the roster was full, and some of the walk ons from last year were still eligible, so they didn't take anybody that year.

The rejection didn't stop me as I knew that I needed time to get better anyways, so I dedicated myself that school year. I came across a video called" how bad do you want it by Eric Thomas." It's funny how I see this video right when I'm about to enter grind mode. It made me wonder and see just how far I could push myself. I just got to college and it is already changing me for the best. I woke up at 5 am to work out then had class from 9-1 M-W-F, and 10-12 T-Th. After my last class, I would go back to the gym and grind again or play some basketball. I was even lucky enough to have a mentor like John Garwood who also allocated his own time to train me. I gave up partying on Thursdays because I knew I needed to work out in the morning. I saved my partying for Fridays and Saturdays. We all need some outlet from our routine or grind. I needed to be structured because if I wasn't then, I wasn't going to grow or remain focused. Everything was set up for me; all I had to do was put in the work.

My sophomore year approached quicker than ever. I had worked all fall, winter, spring, and summer to prepare myself for one day. Once again tryouts were here. I became well known from playing basketball at the rec and most people at the tryouts I had already played against, so I knew their game. It was still a different vibe when playing in front of coaches as opposed to the rec, yet, the nerves disappeared after 5 minutes. I had a great tryout and was the best one there, in my opinion. I scored at will and played 1 on 1 basketball instead of team basketball. I wanted to show off my hard work and that I was the best one there, but I didn't show what they "needed." Once again, I failed and didn't make the team. Can you imagine working all year being the best one on the floor, even reaping compliments from the staff, only to have the coaches tell you that "we were looking for height, good passers and defenders, not a scorer." I couldn't change how tall I was, but in my head, I said anybody can pass and play defense like what the heck. I guess they wanted a drone and not somebody who might try and show up their scholarship players. It was hard to cope with because after the tryout, I was so upbeat about everything. It was as if I took a test that I studied all year for and felt like I got an A when I got an F all because of one step I missed. My friend that made the team, I was better then, but that's my opinion. It hurt even more when guys that knew me before saw me up in the stands but them on the bench as if I wasn't as good as I use to be. I refuse to belittle others or be jealous, so I congratulated them. It's easy to get down on ourselves when we fail or lose, but that is the formula to depression. The frustration I felt was gigantic, but I didn't get bitter or hate the coaches. I just said Good Luck this season; I'll be back next year.

I had two homies which were Kevin Gaines and Marcus Scales who had the same goals as mine and were just as determined. The three of us worked out together and pushed each other constantly. My junior year comes, and I'm ready for another go at making the team. Before the tryout even started, the coach tells us that our roster is full, so we won't be taking anybody. Another year of hard work wasted. It was starting to get to me, how hard I was working, yet it wasn't paying off. I started to wonder if I should give up. My pride was kicking in and I started feeling as if I was too good to keep trying out. The thought of not knowing what would have happened if I gave up would kill me, so my curiosity was larger than my pride. I couldn't let them get the best of me, so I took two weeks off then got back to the grind. Over the summer, I landed an internship, which was great for my career. I woke up at 5 to work out, then went to work at 7 or 8, then after, I would study for the summer classes I was in, then go to sleep and repeat. I was fortunate that the classes were online. I gave up my summer for a better cause, and a better future. I truly believed that hard work breeds success as I have seen it countless times. A thank you to Naruto, giving up was not an option anymore.

My senior year came, and I felt like I was in the best shape of my life. Even the new house I moved into had a basketball court for me to work out in, so I was like this is it. The tryouts came quickly, and as this might be my last chance, I prayed a long message as I needed the inner confidence to eradicate my doubt. I had a good tryout. I did the best I could and had no regrets, but the rest was up to fate. A week goes by, and they were under investigation for something, so they said they weren't taking anybody as of now. So, I still had hope. One day, I see my friend wearing a jersey who also tried out—turns out he made the team. I was happy for him because he worked just as hard as I did, yet it was another failure for me. I had been working out for 4 years, bettering my game each time. I would even play pick up vs the guys on the team, and I would hold my own, so I knew I was good enough—I just needed the chance. I was worrying about too many things out of my control, which caused so much anxiety. Also understand that I was doing engineering schoolwork on top of all this.

Sometimes, we become so engulfed in our goals that we forget the little steps we achieve toward bettering our future. In my head, I was worried about making the team even though I failed to realize that another year of engineering was completed. After finishing my 4th year, I needed a few more classes, which meant I had one more semester to take, but my love for the game was too high, so I decided to take up a minor and just finish in one more year. I spent another year working out even harder especially since I had a basketball court in my backyard. I felt like it was fate for me to keep working out since I was blessed with a court in my backyard.

My super senior year came, and I felt even better about my game. I also had an exam called the fundamentals of engineering coming up, which was the next step for me career-wise. I failed the 1st time before school even started, yet it still didn't distract me from what was in store for me. I knew this was my year to finally make the team and reap the benefits of all my hard work. One of the custodians even asked for my autograph assuming I played on the team as I was working out in the practice facility, so of course I signed. I was practicing for how it would feel when I would actually be on the team. It was justice for me to end my college days on a high note, or so I thought. The training I did for 4 years, waking up at 5 am, bouncing back from failure each time; everything lead up to this moment. When you believe in something so much that everything you did was for a reason, and those reasons were to satisfy this belief, can in all have a very detrimental effect if it doesn't come to be, as your world can turn upside down like mine did. When I found out I didn't make the team for the 5th straight time, it killed me inside. To grind so much and not see any results is defeating. You could ask why it meant so much, when I would most likely only be a practice player. When you do something your whole life, it becomes your identity. To simply restart is not an easy task which is why taking chances is hard for the majority. There was a void missing from high school that I yearned to fill for my ego's sake. I was willing to give up on my goals as what I believed to be my purpose or the path for my future didn't come to fruition. I wanted to blame the coaches for not giving me a chance but they did, it just wasn't in their best interest plus the tides were not in my favor so all I had was myself to reflect on. I prayed and my desires didn't come true. I always wondered why some were born like LeBron James and while there are those born with an illness. I pondered more than just about my own life but life in retrospect.

I had a great path set up. I worked hard, studied harder, treated others positively, even volunteered at a few places yet it felt like I was in an elevator just going downward. I was only 22 years old and everything I worked for and believed in which would happen did not. My whole world was shaking up as my conviction was diminished. I was at a point where I was going to throw my bibles off the cliff but I didn't. It was as if I would throw away everything my past self-had worked hard for. Something told me not to give up or maybe it was the fear of how society would now view me.

I became depressed for a little bit and out of a worse time for this to happen drake releases a new album (drake always brings out the feels). The process of recovery made me feel like a lifeless zombie. To walk around so confused, so broken, just getting by. Not even acting upbeat or putting a façade on, so low, but when you reach the bottom floor the only way is up right?

Eventually I got tired of moping around and feeling like my world was over. I didn't like the basement anyway plus I was fortunate enough to have a good support system and it was them that picked me up through their kind and blunt words of wisdom. Pondering on my life and the faith my support system had, made me reflect on myself even more. I made the decision as to truly realize how I got like this and to understand if there was a reason, I experienced these hardships. I believed in hard work breeds success, yet I wasn't seeing success. I thought that if I can overcome and succeed then I wonder how strong I could become. I decided to challenge my own internal adversary.

The process wasn't a destination but a journey. I began writing as my ego was too high to express my internal feelings, yet writing just seemed to help. I became curious and obsessed with trying to understand the comprehension of who I was but the problem was, I'm not going to understand overnight, so the sadness, pain and suffering were still eminent. I coped with it and tried my best to persevere, how difficult it was. I read books, articles, and blogs. I watched documentaries, TV shows, movies, anything that I felt which was prudent for transcending myself.

I still had to go to school by the way but after a while you put the mask back on. A few days later in one of my classes my professor by the name of Lori Stewart had posted in one of her lectures slides to "rejoice in your suffering". I questioned as to how can me feeling like this be a time to rejoice. The more research and introspection I did, the more it made sense to me.

Romans Chapter 5 Verse 3:4 - Suffering produces perseverance; perseverance, character; and character, hope. It dawned on me as words cut deeper than any blade. I realize that my failures led to my suffering but because I persevered, I was able to overcome that obstacle. When you persevere, you will look back at your old self in aww, because that self will remind you of the pain and sacrifices it took to get to where you are now. The confidence that comes with overcoming a challenge is like that extra topping on a sundae. The confidence added to my character, slowly shaped me, molded me and strengthened me. Despite the trials and tribulations of life, I never gave up hope that a better day would come. I had hope in that what I experienced and learned was for a reason and that I needed to continue to move forward on my path in order to discover that reason. Hope without work is the same as giving up. Be careful as putting too much hope in something without action can be a dangerous deed. Hope with work and a plan can give you something to long for. Don't abandon hope. In all, hope is a good thing and hope never dies until your conviction does.

I began looking into how people handle adversity and the things I found made me understand that I did all I could and that the rest wasn't up to me. It taught me to only worry about things you can control. It made me stronger especially seeing the coaches and how happy I looked to them. It was as if they looked at me and exclaimed how can this guy smile after we rejected him year after year, got to respect it. I realized that they have their own jobs and careers to worry about not my dreams, so why lose myself over that. I had the most important thing in life which was my health and strength and I could still play the game I love. I will say that the coaches were always motivating and vibrant, so I hope my story doesn't portray them negatively because their demeanor and positivity is something that kept me coming back as well plus I'm rooting for my Aztecs every game!

As things began to look up, I was still trying to graduate college, pass my engineering exam, find out who I was in this universe, plan my future and also hone a relationship. It was a lot on my plate but when you are young, emotions are hard to handle for some. A lot was on my mind and I didn't have the space for a relationship at the time yet I was in love so it was a hard choice. It was hard for her to but after a year of being together it was over. I wanted a break to do some soul searching but she said I don't do breaks so I had to do something so painful which was to hurt somebody who has done nothing but great things for you and has a big part of you in their heart. I felt extremely terrible but I knew that if I continued on that I would be going downhill mentally from my own selfish desires, so a pause was necessary from my comfort zone. Two months and a half go by and the feelings of missing her were too hard to let go. As I reach out to her, I learned that she was already in a new relationship. That hit me hard as to how could you move on so fast? It broke my heart even deeper than before which is how she must have felt in the beginning. I probably sound like a hypocrite but aye, what goes around comes around as karma catches up to us all. I also had my engineering exam scheduled in 3 weeks, so it was sarcastically perfect timing. Anyways I take my engineering exam for the 2nd time and fail again. I was also failing in some of my classes during my last semester. I also had to start applying for jobs since my college career was over. So, I failed to make the basketball team 5 times, failed my fundamentals of engineering exam twice, got my heart broken, began having problems paying rent, failed 2 exams in two of my classes and on top of all this, I was having second thoughts on if I even wanted to work as an engineer. Just imagine how I felt. I'm not telling this story to make you feel sorry for me or anything. I just want you to understand my suffering and what catapulted myself to who you know today. Suffering and pain is different to all of us as we aren't as empathetic when we feel somebodies problems aren't real problems. Similar to how tomorrow could be an important day for somebody yet it could also be a regular day to somebody else. We all yearn to achieve our desires and live the way we are accustomed to, so try to understand one another, despite our differences and opinions.

The ups and downs of life were really getting too me. Once the sun came up, a storm was for sure coming the next day. To continue on, I would drink myself to sleep after finishing the day. It felt good temporarily but emptier afterward. I was really at rock bottom. My cousin had failed his CPA exam a few times but then eventually passed so I called him to see how he bounced back. He said "you can give up that's easy but what are you going to tell your kids when they fail that you can just give up, no you need to persevere right now, grab a book and hit it harder 3rd times the charm, get in the best shape ever to make your ex regret losing you, keep working harder no matter how much you fail, I promise your future self will appreciate you for not giving up. You got this I believe in you". After that speech I bought 2 more study guides, created a new workout chart and a schedule on how to apply for jobs. I would not let adversity defeat me.

Through these tough times I figured out my purpose and grew to become an individual that became obsessed with growth. In the end I ended up graduating with a civil engineering degree and a minor in religious studies, passed my fundamentals of engineering exam, lost 15lbs, and was paying all my bills on my own. I want to help others just like how others helped me. During my tough times I began to understand that we all need help and that you never know what you could say to somebody which could help their life. Whatever you are going through, you can handle it, never give up, you may not see the result now but you will see them eventually!

I use to think to myself, was all my hard work for nothing. Even though I never got the chance to play college ball, I still achieved a college level game so when I go to the gym it's just all fun when hooping verse those guys. Playing basketball is good serenity for my heart. I went from being unwanted by college coaches to being the guy everyone wants on their team at the gym. It's all about how you look at things.

When you feel all is lost remembers what remains and continue to rise each and every time. The saying time heals all wounds is correct if you acknowledge yourself. I learned that if it wasn't for the bad times, I wouldn't be who I am today. I learned from not only the positive but the negative as well, as the failures I experienced made me stronger. We rejoice in our sufferings because pain is the best teacher as strength blooms in adversity. Every situation taught me something new. When you replace why is this happening with what is this teaching me, your life changes immediately.

Sometimes we can fall of the track of life and a restart may be necessary as if we kept playing the game in the same manner then we wouldn't be able to defeat it. When we give up it creates a foundation that when things get tough, it's welcoming to take the easy way out or form excuses. These obstacles when forsaken can diminish your spirit. Your inner spirit is powerful but can only take so many attacks. Persevering and being resilient will enhance your character so much that your spirit will be untouchable and along with hope, forms a completed human.

Ironically, I became so in twined in the comprehension of who I was that it made me not think about myself but those out there with no support system. The more people I would help the more positive I felt. The feeling of inspiring, motivating and bringing up another's spirit is what began to fascinate me. I saw the effect that I had by achieving challenging feats and accepting daunting task; it made those think that if Jerald can do it then so can I, which they are correct indeed. I want to help on a global scale, as the things I've learned can help so many people that I cannot reach on my own. I plan one day to reach that dream of being in a position to where I can motivate, inspire and aid in those in need all over the world. When we lead by example, it portrays a flame that is capable of lighting every soul that vividly perceives your illustrations.

I'm happy though with my life. I enjoy doing engineering; I am currently studying for my engineering license. I love playing basketball at the gym and I'm blessed to have endured during tough times. Certain events that caused me so much pain, where I wish it never happened, I'm glad they happened because they helped me grow into who I am today. I feel like I can do anything especially with God on my side.

About the Author

Jerald (25) grew up in beautiful San Diego, CA and as it's a tourist destination, he decided to attend San Diego State University where he earned his Bachelors of Science in Civil Engineering and a minor in Religious Studies. He not only enjoys constructing bridges and structures, but ourselves internally and externally as well. The search for his dreams, the grit and wit of his life contributed to his resilient curiosity about change, the human mind, and our life path. He has studied hundreds of interviews, debates, documentaries, anime, and read countless articles, blogs, books, and anything relevant in which would equip him with invaluable knowledge pertaining to life. His zodiac sign is a cusp of a Cancer and a Leo and he is of house Gryffindor and Stark for all you Harry Potter and Game of Thrones lovers out there.

Stuff He Loves: Basketball, Connect Four, Eating, Music, Ping Pong, Relaxing, Sleeping, Working Out and Working Hard.

www.ingramcontent.com/pod-product-compliance
Lightning Source LLC
Chambersburg PA
CBHW052018070526
44584CB00016B/1808